The Challenge for
School Leaders

THE CONCORDIA UNIVERSITY CHICAGO LEADERSHIP SERIES

An Educational Series from Rowman & Littlefield

Education leaders have many titles and positions in American schools today: professors, K–12 teachers, district and building administrators, teacher coaches, teacher evaluators, directors, coordinators, staff specialists, etc. More than ever, educators need practical and proven educational and leadership resources to stay current and advance the learning of students.

Concordia University Chicago Leadership Series is a unique resource that addresses this need. The authors of this series are award-winning authors and scholars who are both passionate theorists and practitioners of this valuable collection of works. They give realistic and real-life examples and strategies to help all educators inspire and make a difference in school improvement and student learning that get results.

This Leadership Series consists of a variety of distinctive books on subjects of school change, research, completing advanced degrees, school administration, leadership and motivation, business finance and resources, human resource management, challenging students to learn, action research for practitioners, the teacher as a coach, school law and policies, ethics, and many other topics that are critical to modern educators in meeting the emerging and diverse students of today. These books also align with current federal, state, and various association accreditation standards and elements.

Staying current and building the future require the knowledge and strategies presented in these books. The Leadership Series Originator, Daniel R. Tomal, PhD, is an award-winning author who has published over 15 books and 100 articles and studies, and is a highly sought-after speaker and educational researcher. He along with his coauthors provide a wealth of educational experience, proven strategies that can help all educators aspire to be the best they can be in meeting the demands of modern educational leadership.

The Challenge for School Leaders

A New Way of Thinking about Leadership

Ronald Warwick

ROWMAN & LITTLEFIELD
Lanham • Boulder • New York • London

Published by Rowman & Littlefield
A wholly owned subsidiary of
The Rowman & Littlefield Publishing Group, Inc.
4501 Forbes Boulevard, Suite 200, Lanham, Maryland 20706
www.rowman.com

Unit A, Whitacre Mews, 26-34 Stannery Street, London SE11 4AB

British Library Cataloguing in Publication Information Available

Library of Congress Cataloging-in-Publication Data Available

ISBN 978-1-4758-1094-3 (cloth : alk. paper)
ISBN 978-1-4758-1095-0 (pbk.   )
ISBN 978-1-4758-1096-7 (electronic)

Printed in the United States of America

This book is dedicated to Don Gable, a dear friend and colleague for thirty years. We presented many professional-development seminars together, and he designed software programs to assist many graduate students and educators to evaluate their schools. He is a valuable person in my personal and professional life.

Contents

List of Figures

Foreword

As superintendent of schools for twenty-four years in a high-performing suburban district, I have experienced the challenges associated with providing teachers and other staff members with the necessary knowledge and skills to address emerging needs and incorporating what emerging research tells us about learning and teaching. With the "quick fixes" being thrust upon educators from all quarters, the need is greater than ever for a systemic approach to improving education. Dr. Ron Warwick has clearly set forth a way to achieve this goal. In this book he shares his zest for encouraging school leaders to understand and apply the continual-improvement philosophy.

As a public-school teacher and administrator as well as a college professor and department chair, it has been Ron's life-long quest to help his students grow and exceed expectations set before them. As you follow the guidelines laid out in this book, you will learn the essential knowledge and processes that will help you become a leader who makes a difference. Ron Warwick has been that kind of leader, and his wisdom flows throughout the pages of this book. He demonstrates the power of system's thinking through the integration and collaboration of students, staff, and parents to enhance the educational experience.

This book is not for casual reading. Rather it is a thoughtful academic study designed to help school leaders address the problems facing American education with relevant substance. It is a study that helps guide school leaders in understanding and implementing communication, curriculum, instruction, assessment, and statistical data-analysis systems to effect changes in the way we educate our students. It deals with the ways to positively address these critical areas of need in our schools.

Unfortunately the American populace has been bombarded with negatively tainted, oversimplified sound bites relative to high-stakes testing and standardized assessments as the be-all-and-end-all determination of how well our public schools are serving our students. As school leaders, we know education goes far beyond academic assessment that is encapsulated in these oversimplified reports. We as school leaders are responsible for advancing not only the academic development but also the social, emotional, psychological, and physical development of each child. This book shows you how to achieve this goal.

Throughout this book, Dr. Warwick challenges educators by integrating systems and processes through which educators can improve student learning and other developmental needs. We cannot afford to wait to start on the road to continual improvement. This book directs a new way of thinking about school leadership. The challenge is before us. School leaders must create and cause this transformation!

William J. Attea, Ed.D.
Glenview, Illinois

William J. Attea served as superintendent of the Glenview Public Schools in suburban Chicago for twenty-four years. Upon retirement from his superintendent position, he directed Hazard, Young, Attea & Associates for twenty-five years. In this capacity he assisted over four hundred school boards in thirty-four states as a superintendent-search consultant and in school-board and administrative development. During his tenure as superintendent and consultant, Dr. Attea also served as executive director of Suburban School Superintendents for seventeen years. Membership in this organization was limited to one hundred superintendents of high-performing suburban school districts across the United States.

Preface

Our educational system is failing many of our children. Graduation rates in many of our nation's cities are of concern. The diversity of our student special-needs and cultural variations is increasing. Doing more of the traditional strategies such as passing punitive policies and legislation is not working to improve the educational system. Unless school leaders are taught new ways of thinking about our schooling process, our children will continue to experience inferior education opportunities. School leaders must challenge current forces and methods and create new strategies to meet future student needs.

The aim of writing this book is to present a new way of thinking about the schooling process. It is essential that school leaders understand and create new structures and systems to meet the current needs in education. This book demonstrates a continual improvement philosophy and how to understand system elements in the context of this philosophy. The systems addressed are structural variations, communication, curriculum, instruction, and assessment. Also data analysis of instructional strategies and student performance are addressed.

Five chapters have system surveys that allow the faculty to evaluate the implementation of these systems in their school. The complete survey is in appendix A. The gathering of instructional methods and student-performance data is critical for understanding how to improve the instructional system. This statistical data-analysis process is explained in the book.

Many strategies are suggested to involve staff in decision-making processes, curriculum designs, and instructional methods. Appendix B addresses a collaborative decision-making process. As the professional staff become more proficient in these areas, they take on ownership of the continual improvement process. I believe this book will challenge school leaders who truly want to make a difference in the schooling process for their professional staff and students.

Acknowledgments

I have had the opportunity to share my thoughts with many graduate students through the years. I especially wish to thank Josh Reitz, Susan Center, Stephanie Helfand, and Steven Shadel for their feedback and discussion to help me clarify and expand ideas for this book. I also appreciated the expertise of Jennifer Fisher, who edited a number of figures used in the text.

A special thanks to Dr. William Attea, past school superintendent and faculty colleague, whose feedback was written with a bright red pen! I am grateful for the teachers and school administrators who have implemented many of the ideas in this book and proven their effectiveness. Their names are too numerous to mention, but they are truly making a difference in education.

I wish to thank Carlie Wall and Emily Natsios, my editors at Rowman & Littlefield's education division, for their assistance, and Thomas F. Koerner, publisher of the Concordia University's Chicago Leadership Series in Education, for his support.

My wife, Connie, is my greatest support system. She discusses and edits my writings with her thorough and gentle manner.

Introduction

The aim of this book is to encourage and support school leaders with knowledge and tools to collaborate with their faculty members based on the continual-improvement philosophy to improve essential academic systems and student achievement. As the twenty-first century advances, knowledge and technology are advancing as well, and teachers and learners are moving to a more collaborative relationship with an evolving notion of problem-based curriculum through an integration of content areas.

Also, concepts, content, and competencies within our educational system are moving toward criterion reference assessments based on common-core standards. Not only are teachers expected to be competent in their areas of expertise, they need to possess interactive skills to lead work groups and independent learners through project- and problem-based curricula and experiences. Even though teachers may design much of the curriculum to follow sequentially and with direct instructional formats, in time these structures will evolve into integrating other structural options and designs.

As action-research studies in our schools analyze instructional systems, better strategies can develop and more students can benefit from these research findings. Even now, many instructional strategies involve collaborative work groups addressing projects and problems based on realities within our schools and communities. Professional staff-development programs are advancing these teaching strategies and competencies to improve student achievement.

The day has come when grading has little meaning and demonstrating specific competencies based on criterion-referenced assessment systems needs to become the standard used in our educational system.

When a student meets specific evaluation criteria, evidence exists that demonstrates his or her competencies. When a grade is given, it tells us nothing about this student's competencies.

As technology advances, instructional sensitivity addressing individual student-learning styles and interests along with collaborative task-work groups are the new norm within the school setting. Virtual access to knowledge as well as face-to-face instruction in all content fields will blend into a continuous stream for students to call on when needed. After all this is said and done, the leadership role comes down to the knowledge of understanding academic systems and the ability to integrate and continually improve these systems through working collaboratively with the professional staff.

The aim of this educational journey is to understand and implement the continual-improvement philosophy. The method used to achieve this aim is respecting and collaborating with the professional staff and encouraging action research. They are the most valued people who bring continual improvement to life. However, without effective leadership nothing can happen! It is with this mindset that I invite you to study the concepts and contents in the following chapters:

Chapter 1, Continual Improvement, introduces the continual-improvement philosophy, system elements, leadership challenge, and basic statistical-data analysis tools are defined and clarified for the reader.

Chapter 2, An Overview of Essential Systems, introduces the reader to each academic-system concept and specific characteristics within each system.

Chapter 3, Communication System, establishes an integrated network that facilitates cooperation and collaboration to create optimization of system components.

Chapter 4, Curriculum System, clarifies and aligns student expectations throughout the schooling process through variations of curriculum designs.

Chapter 5, Instruction System, determines the methods and structures through which students engage the curriculum.

Chapter 6, Assessment System, gathers and analyzes data to evaluate instructional-strategy effectiveness and student academic performance.

Chapter 7, Professional Behaviors and Values, explores the importance of respect for all participants and maintaining a drive toward continually improving systems for everyone.

Appendix A, School Academic-Systems Improvement Survey, offers the full version of this survey that has been explored in part in previous chapters.

Each academic system in chapters 2 through 6 is assessed with ten items. Each item and system can be analyzed based on the data gathered. The reliability and validity of the assessment instrument has been correlated to student achievement in a study of eighty-one elementary schools. In this study, internal consistency among the five systems ranged from .79 to .94. This indicates a high degree of internal consistent reliability for each system and the academic model as a whole. Also, factor analysis indicates that the items within each system correlate highly enough with each other to form desirable construct validity in the design of the assessment instrument (Sekulich 2000).

The survey responses can be aggregated and displayed in graphic form through statistical charts. Based on this information, school-leadership staff and professional staff can identify the school improvement–planning priorities to be addressed. Each item is given a score of 1 through 9. A mean score of 1.0 through 3.0 is interpreted as the item or system not being implemented consistently. A mean score of 4.0 through 6.0 is interpreted as the item or system being implemented. A mean score of 7.0 through 9.0 is interpreted as the item or system being implemented consistently.

It is recommended that you complete the assessment instrument in appendix A prior to reading the book and then complete the end of each chapter assessment as you read chapters 2 through 6. This will enable you to check your understanding of the material and have a more accurate assessment of each system.

Appendix B, Decision-Making Process, finally, is aimed at the communities and professionals seeking to improve academic systems.

Once an issue of concern is identified through the data-analysis process, this decision-making process offers

1. identification and root-cause analysis
2. an improvement strategies–planning process to determine solutions
3. steps and a flowchart to identify causes
4. steps and a flowchart to a solution-planning process
5. a ranking process and a control analysis of the solutions
6. and a plan-do-study-act cycle, including criteria and a flowchart for implementation.

Continual Improvement

System: Continual-improvement philosophy
System aim: Student learning and achievement
Methodology: Action-research studies

The continual-improvement philosophy is a simple concept that is able to be implemented if we focus on what should be most valued. The concept of getting better at what we value, and being committed to these values, is not a new idea. However, one has to value the right things and continually improve in the knowledge and behavior that reflects, grows, and sustains these values.

As one transfers this continual-improvement philosophy to one's professional life, one must determine the most important components that are valued within the profession. In education, people are the most important component and each person is of value. This puts our profession apart from most "production-centered" systems. The aim of the schooling process is to add value to each and every person socially, intellectually, and emotionally.

People are both the means and the ends of our efforts and the ones on whom the leader depends to achieve the aim of our schooling process. The affirmation of each person's value is important not only in words but also in a leader's actions, through sharing information and decision making, designing and integrating curriculum, improving instructional strategies, assessing instructional methods, and improving our social and academic performance.

As each person contributes to the improvement of the schooling process, a leader is challenged by how he or she can help improve each player's respective knowledge, creative-thinking and problem-solving skills, and talents to add value to enhance everyone. Only when each person recognizes that everyone is in the game, and is contributing to and gaining from the system, can everyone win.

CONTINUAL-IMPROVEMENT MODEL

The continual-improvement philosophy is the foundation on which professional staff collaboration is built and improves various systems within the educational organization. It is essential to understand the academic systems and the components within each of these systems. The system components are elements that work together to achieve the aim of the system. The aim of a system is the purpose for which the system exists and drives every decision made within the system.

SYSTEM COMPONENTS

System components consist of the following elements:

System: identification of the system being discussed and analyzed
System aim: the purpose for why the system exists
Methods to achieve the aim: the processes used to achieve the aim
Criteria to assess the success of methods used to achieve the aim: determined standards
Data gathered from the methods used: process data to be analyzed
Data gathered from the results of the methods used: product data to be analyzed
Analysis of methods and results data: basis for what needs to be improved
Evaluation of methods and results data: decisions to improve performance
Design of continual-improvement interventions: changes to improve process and performance results

Implementation of improvement interventions: interventions to improve process and performance results

Continue the cycle of improvement: a new way of thinking for the work place

Another value that drives a leader is the belief that everyone should be challenged to think creatively and take appropriate risks and solve problems. In order for this belief to become a reality, the instructional staff needs planning time each day to discuss, analyze, and determine strategies for improvement. Without time built into the day for professional collaboration, the improvement process falters. Providing time for professional-staff collaboration aims to improve the quality of life for each person through enhancing knowledge, competencies, and commitment to the aim of the schooling process. How can this aim be addressed and achieved if time is not given to it?

Every leader of an educational organization needs to convey the joy of learning. This is the culture and climate a leader should be creating and sustaining throughout the educational organization. The continual-improvement philosophy should be demonstrated in every step taken and discussed within and outside the educational system. One must "walk the talk" and make continual improvement a way of life—a new way of thinking (Deming 1994) (see figure 1.1).

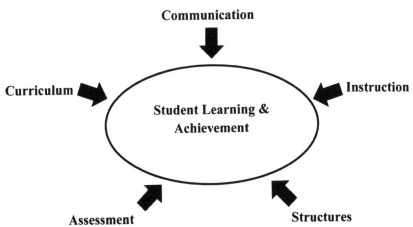

Figure 1.1. *Aim of the Academic Systems: Student Learning and Achievement*

The academic continual-improvement model consists of five essential systems that are addressed in this text to enable educators to improve student learning and achievement: (1) structures and elements, (2) communication, (3) curriculum, (4) instruction, and (5) assessment. As each finger is part of a hand and adds to its optimum multiple functions, each of the five systems is part of the academic continual-improvement model and adds to the achievement of its aim: to improve student critical thinking, learning, and achievement.

An assessment instrument in appendix A is provided to assist in determining baseline data for each system within the academic continual-improvement model. Based on the data gathered, the school leadership team can determine the priorities to be addressed. As these priorities are identified, they can be written into the school-improvement plan, and resources can be allocated to support staff development and other needs to meet the aim of schooling process and student achievement.

LEADERSHIP CHALLENGE

Thinking is a human quality; it is what makes us unique. The challenge before educational leaders is to create a different way of thinking about leadership in order to move an educational organization to its highest level of performance and to better meet the needs of the people it serves. Four areas of thinking that educators need to address are application, analysis, evaluation, and synthesis (Bloom 1956; *Webster's New Collegiate Dictionary* 1980):

> *Application* is the act of putting previous knowledge to use in a new setting. Application of knowledge and experience in new and different situations is essential if innovations and interventions are to occur to improve any schooling process and performance result.
> *Example*: Using instructional strategies that have been successful in the past with a different group of students with whom these strategies have not been implemented and assessing the effectiveness.
> *Analysis* is the separation of a whole into its parts, an examination of each element of this complex entity, and understanding their relationships. Analysis is concerned with understanding the relationships be-

tween and among its components within the context being studied. Each element in a system has its impact on every other element in the system and the performance results of that system.

Example: Giving a problem to a group of students who have never heard or seen this problem, having them analyze what might be the causes of this problem, and explaining how these causes might be related to each other.

Evaluation is the determination of the significance or worth of a process and performance result. Evaluation is essential to assess strategies being used and determine which strategy needs improvement or to be eliminated to achieve the aim of the process and performance result. Evaluation judges if a system process and a performance result is acceptable or desirable.

Example: Give a group of students a product such as a set of house plans and the criteria used by the village planning committee to judge if the plans are acceptable for approval to issue a building permit. The students also have been taught how to evaluate house plans using these criteria in the past.

Synthesis (Creating) is putting together the composition or combination of parts or elements so as to form a new whole . . . integrating and creating a new way of thinking. . . . Synthesis is the creative act of developing new ideas and strategies to advance teaching and learning and creating implementations and interventions to achieve the aim.

Example: Given four roof structures that did not withstand one hundred mile per hour winds and were destroyed, design a roof structure that will stand up against one hundred mile per hour winds.

As a leader assesses any application, he or she observes its current implementation methods and results. This is the starting point of any improvement process. If a situation is deemed to need improvement, the process begins. The first step is to define the system and clarify the aim of the system. Then data are gathered from the process and analyzed. After a leader and staff complete the process analysis, the next step is to evaluate what is or is not working to achieve the aim. The evaluation process enables the team to determine whether or not a change is needed to improve the process. Once the evaluation is complete, synthesis is needed to create and implement a plan to improve the process. As a process is improved, the entire system improves.

The cognitive process of synthesis is what leadership is all about! It is the responsibility of a leader to involve the professional staff in bringing all parts together (synthesize) to improve the processes and results for everyone. A leader works with the people in the school to continually improve all systems to achieve the aim of the school. It is the leader's responsibility to integrate different options within each system in order to maximize its contribution to the whole, and for everyone to benefit as a result.

Analysis is interpreted as "understanding options" in the system; evaluation is interpreted as determining the best strategies to improve the system; synthesis is interpreted as "creating integrations and interventions" to implement system improvement and putting these new ideas into action, and the cycle goes on and on. The integration of these four cognitive functions is essential for a leader's understanding of options and integrations and for creating and implementing interventions for the future.

Understanding one's options in any context is essential to discerning which options are desirable within a particular context. Then, and only then, can a leader and the professional staff make an appropriate decision. This continual-improvement philosophy requires a new way of thinking about academic improvement for each educator. Although some system options are mentioned in these chapters, these options do not include all the possibilities and are only intended to bring to the reader's mind ideas of what may be possible in the future.

STATISTICAL-DATA ANALYSIS

At the heart of any attempt to improve any system or part of any system within the school, the data-gathering process needs to be agreed upon and implemented. This data-gathering process needs to address the methods (implementing strategies) and the outcomes (expectations) of the system and, in the end, evaluate the quality (effectiveness) of the system itself. The type of data gathered generally is of a quantitative and/or qualitative nature.

Quantitative research: (scientific approach) numerical data, objective, hypothesis and variables, statistical analysis of data, natural/contrived setting, accepts/rejects the hypothesis.

Qualitative research: (naturalistic approach) natural setting, involved, study is independent, studies theory/concept, hypothesis not essential, descriptive data analysis to draw conclusions.

Mixed-method research: integration of quantitative and qualitative methodology.

Action research: a process of solving problems and making improvements.

Action research is different from quantitative and qualitative research but has characteristics of both. An action researcher utilizes an appropriate intervention to collect and analyze data and to implement actions to address educational issues. Action research is suitable for educators as a practical process because it does not require elaborate statistical analysis or lengthy narrative explanations but is more concerned with solving a problem in an efficient and feasible manner.

Also, while traditional research methods are much more concerned with relating findings to other settings or populations, action research is more concerned with improvements within the context of the study, such as in a school setting. Therefore, action research is often called *practitioner* or *school-based* research. Action research differs from quantitative and qualitative studies in that it is more direct in its purpose. Since the goal of action research is to solve a given problem and make improvements, action researchers rely less on scientific inquiry and inductive reasoning and more on reflection and practicality and feasibility of addressing a problem.

Action research is often considered a process as much as a research methodology. Therefore, this research is distinguished from other research methodologies because of the collaborative effort of the researcher in working with others and developing action plans to make improvements. This process is concerned with systematic collection of data, which are analyzed and fed back to the professional staff so that action plans can be systematically developed.

A final distinguishing feature of action research is the researcher's use of various interventions (activities) that become the mechanisms for the research itself. In other words, the intervention becomes the object of the research—and a possible solution to the identified problem—if the data analysis supports the positive outcomes on the intervention (Tomal 2010).

Quantitative data, being numerical, can immediately be entered into a software program; however, qualitative data may have to be numerically coded before it can be entered into the software-analysis system. In either case, these types of data can be analyzed using statistical control charts. Control-chart characteristics are explained in the following pages (Creswell 1998; Wheeler 1992).

Statistical control charts are used to analyze system data to determine if system improvement has occurred. Also, control charts determine common and special causes of system variation. Common causes of variation are due to the variables within the system itself, on an ongoing daily basis. If all the variation in the system is on or within the upper and lower control limits, the system is considered in statistical control. This statement is a factual condition and not an evaluative conclusion.

Upper and lower control limits are plus and minus three standard deviations above and below the mean (average) of the system data being analyzed. The evaluation of the data analysis is decided by asking if the control-chart analysis is acceptable to the people implementing the system. See the first control chart below, Eagle High School (figure 1.2), which shows a system in statistical control, and the second, Hawk Middle School (figure 1.3), which shows a system not in statistical control.

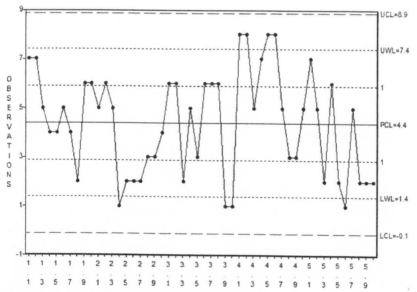

Figure 1.2. Faculty Evaluation of Eagle High School

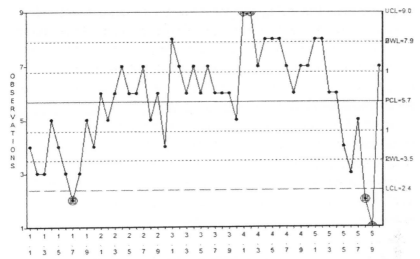

Figure 1.3. Faculty Evaluation of Hawk Middle School

As indicated in the Eagle High School chart, the system is in statistical control, and all the variation is determined by the system itself. In this case, the professional staff decide whether the data are acceptable or not. If the analysis determines the data are acceptable, no action is needed. This system, if left alone, will continue to produce the same results within a very small variance, time after time. If the data analysis is not acceptable, the professional staff must start the process of planning interventions to improve the system.

In the Hawk Middle School control chart, special causes of variation are identified (1.7, 4.2, 4.3, 5.8, 5.9); they go beyond the upper and/or lower control limits and need to be investigated. After investigation, the professional staff decide whether or not further action is needed. In either case, the special causes need to be addressed and removed in order to determine the normal variation of the system under study.

The reason the special causes need to be addressed is that these causes are not random and are not part of the normal system variation and do not allow the staff to understand what the normal variation of the system being studied is until they are removed. Only after the special causes are removed can the system reflect its normal random variation, and at that point the system is within statistical control and the system can now be judged to be acceptable or not acceptable. Once this is achieved, the analysis stated as shown in figure 1.2 above now applies.

In this Hawk Middle School control chart, the professional staff are recording their implementing of the fifty best practices of academically high-performing schools. The data show that some points are above and below the control limits. In this case (4.2, 4.3) being above the upper control limit is positive. Being below (1.7, 5.8, 5.9) the lower control limit is not positive and identifies items that need to be addressed in order to understand and analyze the overall system.

By investigating and removing the special causes, the system can then be recalculated and determined to be in or out of statistical control. If the system is in statistical control, all the variation in the system is due to random variation within the system itself and not the result of any special cause. What is wonderful is that there are software programs available today that can create control charts for data analysis within seconds and can be learned within minutes (Warwick 1995, chap. 5).

It is important that the school community gather and analyze data to implement the improvement efforts of the staff. Data are gathered on system aims such as reading comprehension, decoding skills, math computation, sentence writing, higher-level thinking, problem solving, and many other valued learning criteria. The data are analyzed using statistical programs such as system-process control charts to understand the effectiveness of the instructional method and student performance results.

System-process control charts help the staff understand the instruction-system activity and determine if the instructional process is predictable in the future. Based on the data being produced, the principal and faculty know if the instructional process being used is acceptable or if improvements need to be made. The data analysis is able to identify areas of concern in the process, and the principal and faculty know specific areas in the process that need further investigation. This type of data analysis is essential to improving each instructional process.

Figure 1.4 shows an example of a system not in "statistical control" because some of the points in the population are not within the upper and lower control limits. Notice that students #10 and #19 are outside the upper control limit and, therefore, make this population out of control and the system unpredictable in the near future. In this case, the teacher needs to investigate the "out of control points" and determine what needs to be done.

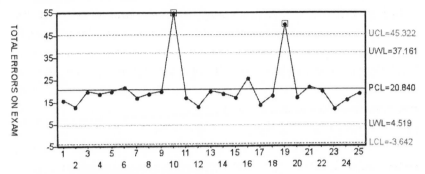

Figure 1.4. **English-Writing Assessment**

Different options may be addressed such as student tutoring, student placement into a study group, direct support from home on additional homework, teacher monitoring of homework, and peer assistance. Students #10 and #19 cannot be ignored if this situation is to improve and the system is to become stable and predictable in the near future. These two student cases are special causes of variation and must be addressed in order to improve the system.

Figure 1.5 shows an example of a system in "statistical control" because all the points in the population are within the upper and lower control limits, which make the system predictable in the near future. In this case, the teacher need not look at any single point in the population and needs to address the system itself as to whether it is meeting expectations or not.

If the system is acceptable to the teacher, nothing need be done and the system will maintain itself with some small degree of variation in the future. If the teacher is not satisfied with the system results, some type of intervention needs to be introduced into the system to improve

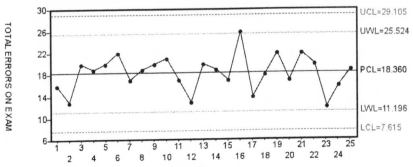

Figure 1.5. **English-Writing Assessment**

it. This might be where the teacher and students discuss the system re-sults and decide some intervention strategies that might be introduced and studied to determine if they improved the system results.

The method of data analysis used by most schools is *normal-distribution data analysis*, and the data come from the testing com-pany normed against different standards, local and national. This data analysis is helpful in showing trends and general types of information; however, much of these data is not helpful with respect to analyzing instructional strategies and does not lend itself to criterion-referenced assessment methods. Much of the data being collected in schools today are of little use for student academic improvement and analyzing in-structional strategies within the instructional system.

Student-results data tell us what the students did on the test, but they do not help us analyze the methods needing improvement. Test results record the end results, not the analysis of the ineffective instructional process used. Also, normal statistical analysis does not let us identify the common and special causes of variation in the system data that control-chart statistical analysis does identify. Normal statistical-data analysis includes all the points in a population within three standard de-viations from the mean and does not identify points that can be outside this normal range, which can be identified when control-chart analysis is performed on the data.

This distinction is critical for proper analysis of system data to de-termine stability and potential improvement of the system. Only when the special causes of variation can be identified and removed can the professional staff understand the normal variation of the system being studied. Once this analysis is completed and special causes are ex-plained and removed, the system is now in statistical control and can be analyzed as to its acceptability. The gathering and analysis of instruc-tional-process data and student test-results data using control charts are essential to the improvement process and impossible without it.

DEFINITION OF TERMS

System is a group of related elements (processes) integrated to ac-complish a purpose.

Process is a grouping of concurrent tasks directed at accomplishing a particular outcome.

Mean is the average of the system data.

Standard deviation is the concentration or dispersion of the data around the mean within specific limits. Normal dispersion limits are 68 percent of the population within one standard deviation, 95 percent of the population within two standard deviations, and almost 100 percent of the population within three standard deviations.

Variation is the range and dispersion of individual system events around the average in a process or number of processes.

Range is the difference between the highest and lowest values in a system or subset of a system.

Dispersion is the concentration of points around the system average.

Control limits are statistical measures of the upper and lower limits within which variation of individual events range (+3 SD and –3 SD).

Statistical control is a characteristic of a process in which variation is random and on or within the upper and lower control limits (between +3 SD and –3 SD).

Common cause of variation is a reason for random process variation that is predictable in the near future. A common cause of variation is within the control limits.

Special cause of variation is a reason for process variation that is neither random nor predictable. It leads to variation outside the control limits.

Tampering is acting on a common cause of variation as if it were a special cause and making the system worse. This action means that the staff does not understand the proper analysis process and importance of normal variation of the system (Deming 1994).

Variation is the dispersion of values in a system. Dispersion is determined by the range, mean (average), and standard deviation of the values of the system. The range is the difference between the highest and lowest values of the system data. Adding the values of the system data and dividing the sum by the number of values in the system determine the average. The standard deviation is determined by the dispersion of values around the average of the system.

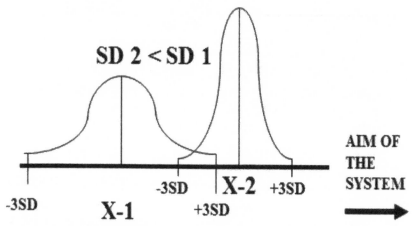

Figure 1.6. *System Improvement*

Understanding the dispersion of a system helps us analyze its variation. The more control (less variation or dispersion) in a system, the better the capability to improve the system. Improving the system is defined as moving the average toward the aim of the system and reducing the dispersion of the system around the new average. Both of these criteria are necessary to improving any system. Figure 1.6 demonstrates the system mean of the data moving toward the aim and the variation (standard deviation/dispersion) of the data decreasing around the new mean.

Figure 1.7 displays points with common causes and special causes of variation. The common-cause variation is within the upper and lower control limits, and the special-cause variation is above and below the control limits.

UPPER CONTROL
LIMIT (+3 SD)

AVERAGE X

LOWER CONTROL
LIMIT (-3 SD)

SPECIAL CAUSES
OF VARIATION

COMMON
CAUSES OF
VARIATION

SPECIAL CAUSES
OF VARIATION

Figure 1.7. *Control Chart*

Decreasing variation is one of the criteria necessary to improve a system. Figure 1.8 demonstrates reducing the variation because of the

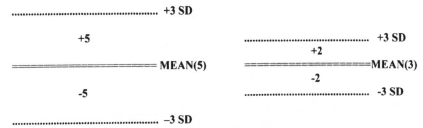

Figure 1.8.   Reducing the Mean and Variation for Absent Students

decreased range in the new distribution and, therefore, meeting the second criteria for system improvement.

In figure 1.8 both criteria for system improvement are demonstrated with respect to students being absent each period of the school day. The first figure shows the mean of five students absent per period with a variation of plus and minus five; and the second figure shows the new mean at three and the variation being reduced to plus and minus two. Therefore, both criteria for system improvement are demonstrated as being met in this example.

An example of trend-data description and analysis is given in figure 1.9. The means of each grade level is 0.2 higher in the research group than in the control group. The lower control limit in each of the experimental groups is higher than in each of the control groups. Also, the upper control limits are higher in each of the experimental groups than in each of the control groups. Also, the standard deviation in all three grades meets the criterion of decreasing around the mean in the experimental groups more than in the control groups. Therefore, both criteria of the mean moving toward the aim and the standard deviation decreasing around the new mean are satisfied in all three grade levels. This defined system improvement at all three grade levels.

GRADE	**EXPERIMENTAL GROUP**				**CONTROL GROUP**			
	MEAN(PCL)	UCL	LCL	U-L	MEAN(PCL)	UCL	LCL	U-L
1st GRADE	1.8	2.5	1.1	1.4	1.6	2.5	0.7	1.8
2nd GRADE	2.8	3.6	2.0	1.6	2.6	3.6	1.7	1.9
3rd GRADE	3.9	4.7	3.1	1.6	3.7	4.6	2.8	1.8

Figure 1.9.   Reading Comprehension Data

READING-COMPREHENSION DATA ANALYSIS

It is clear that the experimental group data indicate that the *small-group reinforcement* method of instruction is better than not hewing to this type of strategy. At every grade level the data indicate the experimental student groups did better than the control student groups. This reading strategy should be continued and recommended for an expanded implementation throughout the school.

READING-COMPREHENSION RECOMMENDATION

Small-group reading reinforcement, as a reading strategy, should be implemented throughout the reading program at all grade levels in the school. Planning for this implementation should be discussed at the building-instructional-improvement team meeting as soon as possible, and a planning team needs to be assigned.

Quantitative and qualitative data can be analyzed through the use of various charts. As different types of instructional interventions are introduced into the system, the faculty can determine whether or not the interventions improve the results. It is through this process of instructional analysis and intervention that continual improvement of the instructional system is achieved. As the methods of instruction improve, student achievement improves.

The system-data analysis process is reviewed in the following:

1. Identify the system being analyzed.
2. Determine the criteria to be assessed.
3. Determine criteria behavioral indicators.
4. Identify the type of data to be collected to address criteria.
5. Determine the method of data gathering.
6. Determine the type of data analysis.
7. Gather the data.
8. Run the control chart.
9. Analyze the control-chart data.
10. Draw conclusions from the data analysis.
11. Recommend improvement interventions based on the conclusions.

CHAPTER 2

An Overview of Essential Systems

System: Academic systems
System aim: Academic-systems implementation and integration
Methodology: Professional-staff communication and collaboration

STRUCTURAL VARIATIONS

The structural variations that exist throughout our nation's schools are limitless. Our schools group students in every grade and age pattern that one can imagine. Different grades are combined at the pre-K to pre-K–3 levels, fourth-through-sixth levels, fifth-through-eighth levels, sixth-through-ninth levels, sixth-through-twelfth levels, and countless other combinations. Often these structures are not based on needs of students but rather on the community's space and financial considerations.

As we move deeper into the twenty-first century, the face of schooling is changing before our eyes. Every day we witness new variations of educational opportunities such as home, virtual, hybrid, face-to-face, public- and private-charter, magnet, and many other types of schooling yet to come in the future. As the digital world unfolds, traditional classrooms as we know them today may no longer exist. Today students are able to attend classes and view topics electronically (Adams 2013). Also, students have the opportunity to use interactive systems to discuss ideas and continually interact with other students and teachers.

The digital age is in full swing, and we have the capacity to communicate with anyone instantly and electronically access any research and general information on almost any topic at the touch of our fingers. These technical changes are changing the role of teaching as well. Teachers are becoming resource and discussion leaders for small groups and individual students. Large class lectures will no longer be necessary because the lectures can be given on electronic systems and recalled when needed by students. Teachers can be on call to advise and guide a number of students and refer each student to a contact person and database if more advanced information or knowledge is needed to support each student's learning and academic growth.

Not only are the structures and options of gathering information changing before our eyes, the process of instruction itself is being restructured away from highly structured lesson-plan sequences to problem- and project-based learning. The ownership of critical thinking and problem-solving systems is now shifting to students learning these processes through engagement in real-life issues, and teachers are responsible for asking excellent questions and being resources for problem-solving systems rather than giving answers (Project Lead the Way, February 2, 2014).

Also, as students become more knowledgeable about these new methodologies of instruction, the opportunities for student-centered, self-paced, and self-directed learning become possible. These teaching methodologies are moving across the nation, and many teachers are re-educating themselves to meet these demands (San Francisco State University, February 2, 2014).[1]

As excellent instructional options are made more available, more students are benefiting from quality teaching provided online and through interactive systems that present collaboration with others in learning. This provides almost every student an opportunity to access quality instructional strategies and materials as well as optional teaching styles that can meet individual needs in a timely manner.

Today professional staff no longer have to attend workshops and conferences to gain new knowledge and meet certification requirements. Rather, they can attend electronic classes and meet assessment criteria online. When online resources are utilized appropriately, significant savings on travel, lodging, meals, and extensive materials can be realized. These training sessions can also be attended on the learner's own time with no time taken away from the work day (iNACOL 2011).

An example of professional-development education conducted in this manner is the implementation of the State of Illinois teacher-evaluation legislation passed in January 2010. The State of Illinois' Performance Evaluation Reform Act (PERA) integrates student-academic performance into the evaluation of teachers and administrators. In order to evaluate any teacher or administrator, one must attend and pass the online PERA training modules (Illinois State Board of Education, January 2010).

Educational structures need to be designed to meet the future needs of teachers and students. In this digital age students need more time for discussion and specific explanation on concepts and topics of interest. As general information is disseminated electronically, small study groups and individual research studies need to be guided by teachers. School buildings are becoming digital- and discussion-resource centers, and teachers are becoming advisers and resource discussion leaders.

The days of large group lectures in person are limited, and small study groups on specific objectives and issues are what building designs need to address. Therefore, building space must be flexible and open to any option of instruction needed at any given moment in time. As the electronic age advances, wireless systems allow flexibility in accessing instructional materials, and flexible space for student-instructional grouping patterns need to be designed in future buildings to address the various grouping options on an at-need basis.

STRUCTURAL INTEGRATIONS

The younger student may need more direct teacher contact, but as a student progresses through the educational system, the degree of virtual-learning options increases, and as one moves into adulthood, much of the educational system is available through virtual systems with minimal face-to-face contact and only on an as-needed basis. As one reviews the literature on virtual schools in the United States, it is clear that each state is moving to integrate online learning with face-to-face learning to some degree (Cuban 2013).

As states review the research on virtual-learning systems, it is still unclear which claims can be validated (Headden 2013; iNACOL 2006). What comes next can only be left to the imagination, but

schooling as we know it is moving more toward a contextual prob-
lem- and project-based learning model and is requiring application
and evidence of knowledge learned.

ISSUES TO BE ADDRESSED

As these blended integration models of instruction grow throughout our
nation, some issues need to be addressed.

Seat time versus competency-based learning: Electronic time on task
needs to take the place of seat time as we know it today. Actually,
electronic time needs to give way to process and performance criteria being demonstrated, as future educational systems become more
flexible and appropriate in meeting the needs of individual students.
As instruction is individualized, different students can move at different rates and levels of knowledge through learning modules.

Time on task is not the measure of learning and is not appropriate in this modern age. Essential competencies need to be taught
and learned, and advancement must be based on assessed knowledge, not time in class (Warwick 1995, chaps. 8–9). Also, the
curriculum is integrating problem- and project-based experiences
to meet standards and moving away from a top-down teacher-
directed methodology.

The traditional sequence of teachers directing textual knowledge
followed by noncontextual applications is evolving into student-
centered, context-based problem and project learning. Students
meeting criterion reference-based assessments on agreed-upon
levels of thinking and standards are the expectations in today's
schooling process.

Instructional options open to every student: All methods of instruction can be available for each student. Teaching is not only about
how to access knowledge but also how to use this knowledge effectively. Each student begins at a different level of learning and
learns at a different rate and through a different style. Various
options of instructional strategies can be made available to meet
these individual needs in a timely manner.

Blended-interaction sessions: Students need to interact face-to-face, virtually and in person. As schooling and working settings integrate blended systems of interaction, students should have opportunities to experience these methods and strategies early in their schooling. These experiences can provide students with the opportunities to develop relational and social skills needed to foster collaborative skills for all phases of life.

Learning independent of age and grade levels: As individual assessments and different instructional strategies are developed, students are able to learn and advance in knowledge based on demonstrated competencies and should not be limited by age or grade-level categories. Multiage and multigrade groupings of students within reasonable variations may be the norm as is true in many classrooms today. Even though there is age variation within two to three years on average within many classrooms today, the variation in the student-learning groups is becoming more variable and diverse.

Curriculum integration of concepts and topics: Subject content areas of knowledge need to be integrated to enable students to learn multidimensional aspects of information on various concepts and topics. This allows students to integrate knowledge and have a deeper and broader view of analysis to enhance understanding and problem identification as well as create options for solutions. The curriculum needs to be more reality based in problems, projects, and issues that invite the student into today's world and reflect on the history leading to these realities. Then the student can be asked to suggest creative solutions and, if possible, test these solutions.

Variable instructional strategies integrated to address multiple learning styles: Students need to access knowledge of concepts and topics through various strategies of teaching, which includes modes of instruction and styles of learning. The virtual-knowledge base allows this to happen as each student needs it.

Teacher's role as knowledge mentor and adviser: Teachers are going to lead many small-group discussions and give individual tutoring sessions as their role develops in the future. Students receive most of their information and knowledge through visual and written sources via multimedia systems. Teacher expertise is essential for student interaction and is shared mostly through small-group and individual interactions online and face-to-face. The problem- and project-based instructional model is consistent with this methodology and supports the new teacher-student relationship.

Academic competency versus academic grades: Academic grades are becoming meaningless. Assessment systems can determine student competencies and advancement in levels of knowledge based on meeting competency criteria at various levels. The common-core standards are the minimum baseline for future assessment systems. As content and concept competencies are assessed through various documented problem solutions, project completions, application competencies, and other portfolio requirements, grades do not serve any purpose. Student evidence is the norm for advancing in levels of knowledge and application and future challenges.

Teacher collaboration and integration of content knowledge: Teachers can integrate content knowledge into thematic units to enable students to multidimensionally analyze information and integrate viewpoints for better understanding of information and data. Integrating various knowledge sources from different perspectives expands the student's thinking in areas being studied.

Professional staff and community members leading action research to improve academic systems: Professional staff and community members need to be involved in action research of the curriculum-instruction-assessment cycle to continually improve the instructional processes and use student feedback as an element to do so. Everyone in the school setting is a member of the team to improve the schooling process, and everyone benefits when this is the aim of the school. An organic curriculum with a reality-based instructional process can integrate the entire community into the continual improvement system and energizes the entire school community.

Parent, community member, professional staff, and student cooperation and collaboration: As school communities become digitally integrated, communication networks can be used to gather input data and inform everyone on many relevant issues. Additionally, open communication networks can be used to conference, get feedback, evaluate, and improve many aspects of the school system.

Parents and other community members integrated into the school-improvement process: As the blended virtual and person-to-person options are integrated, many contributors are going to be involved in the schooling process and have input into the improvement process. Professional leaders need to create multiple systems of communication and feedback to serve all elements of the learning community.

As we assess the many variations of our student-grouping structures and blended instructional-delivery options, the concern that needs to be addressed in all of these systems is the integration of planning, implementing, and assessing the curricular-instructional-assessment systems. For this to occur, leaders must design and implement communication structures that enable professional staff to participate in every phase of curriculum development, instructional design, data gathering and analysis, and continual improvement of the academic systems for our students.

Understanding the curriculum, instruction, and assessment systems and how they are integrated and continually improved determines the quality of the academic program of any schooling process. Our schools are a reflection of our community, and this partnership needs to be nourished and developed continually. There is no reason the lines of communication and opportunities for collaboration cannot be used to benefit the students in our care. Each student needs all of us in the community to provide the best support to enable his or her success.

The decision-making process suggested in appendix B brings parents and community members into the school-improvement process and builds positive community relations in a meaningful way. Without community support, any school is not able to be the best it can be and serve the community needs to its fullest.

ACADEMIC-SYSTEM INTEGRATION

A *system* is defined as a series of components, functions, and activities within an organization that work together to achieve the purpose (*aim*) of the organization. Each component works together with other components to benefit the components and the system.

An example of a system is an orchestra. An orchestra is a group of people who play different instruments blended together to create music. All the members of the group are there to support each other. The conductor blends the music of the players to benefit the whole group. No one plays as loudly as he or she can to be inappropriately noticed. Music, not noise, is the aim, and each component of the orchestra blends its sound with the sound of other components to achieve the aim (Warwick 1995). This interdependence between and among system components is essential to understand for the system aim to be possible.

The school instructional budget–allocation process can be used as another example to make this point. In many school districts, the instructional budget is controlled by the school or central-office administrators. Often the building professional staff have little or no decision-making power in allocating finances and determining spending priorities. The money for each building is assigned by central office and then distributed by the school administrator for each grade level or department, and that is the end of the story.

When a leader understands the instructional-budgeting system and applies the continual-improvement philosophy to it, he or she believes in the collaborative decision-making process as well as respecting the professional staff. Also, the leader understands the interdependence between and among the instructional-system elements and how all these system elements work together to achieve the aim of the budget-allocation process.

The leader starts the instructional budget–allocation process by stating the total amount allocated for the school's instructional budget and asking each teaching department, team, and grade level to submit its budget for the coming school year. Each group representative brings its budget request to the building-leadership meeting and explains and defends its request. As the requests are reviewed and debated, and teacher groups revise their requests, the amounts come closer to the allocated amount.

After a number of meetings, the budget allocation is reached, and each representative agrees with the final allocations and supports the expenditures. In this manner each team understands where allocations are being spent, and the professional-staff priorities are being addressed. The school community is assured that funds are being spent appropriately, and the process is open to anyone for review. When a leader and staff are able to identify the *system*, state its aim, determine methods to achieve the aim, and assess the effectiveness of its results, everyone benefits.

Again, the four key elements of understanding any system are (1) defining the system, (2) clarifying the aim (purpose) of the system, (3) determining the methods by which the aim is achieved, and (4) assessing the results of the system. Leaders need to implement and integrate these four essential systems to create a highly academic-performing school. These systems are (1) a linked communication system, (2) an integrated curriculum system, (3) a variable-strategies instructional system, and (4) a statistically based assessment system. These systems are addressed in depth in subsequent chapters, and an introduction to each is presented.

LINKED-COMMUNICATION SYSTEM

The aim of an effective communication system is to integrate knowledge from relevant participants within various levels of an organization to improve its processes and achieve its goals. These collaborative concepts allow the communication system to work more efficiently and effectively.

The administrative leadership of the school structures the school day to facilitate cooperative-planning time for the instructional teams, which gives them time to design integrated academic programs for the students. Through common academic planning time, these instructional teams discuss school issues and suggest improvement strategies for overall academic improvement of the school program.

Also, the administrative staff design the communication system to enable weekly meetings for teacher representatives from the instructional teams to meet with the building administrator at the building-leadership meeting to discuss programs and school issues to improve and achieve the school aim. It is through a linked and layered communication system that any school staff is able to deal with all the issues needing attention for continual academic improvement.

These weekly meetings can be scheduled one day after student school hours or after a shortened student scheduled day. Many schools have alternative bell schedules to create an additional period at the end of the student school day for professional staff and administrative meetings.

As team representatives and the school administrator meet weekly, minutes of these meetings are taken and shared with all the staff in a timely manner (the next day). The team representatives discuss and clarify the minutes for the staff at a team meeting. Because of the open discussion of all important issues, the staff is involved and takes ownership of the academic functions of the school program. The effectiveness of the academic program depends on an effective communication system and cannot achieve its aim without it (see figure 2.1).

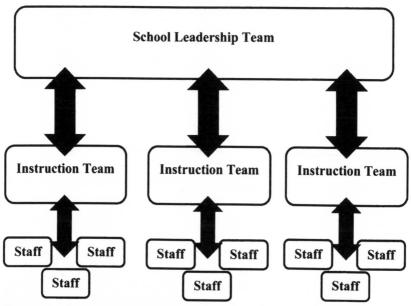

Figure 2.1.   Communication-System Linkages

INTEGRATED-CURRICULUM SYSTEM

The *curriculum system* is what the academic local community members, professional staff, and school community members value and teach their children. The curriculum system is based on a common core of state standards and should reflect professional-staff priorities, professional-organization standards, and community values. The curriculum is driven by the values of the people, and it is the heart of the academic program.

The professional staff align the curriculum to assure the local community that the students receive an excellent learning experience.

The curriculum is vertically layered as well as horizontally integrated to assure the proper sequence, scope, and depth for each student's learning experience. Through the integration of these various sources, the staff build the curriculum of the school. Once the curriculum is in place, the staff identify criteria used to determine student performance on each of the curricular expectations. Based on these criteria, the staff can determine the effectiveness of the academic program as well as the student competencies.

Curriculum effectiveness is determined through gathering data and analyzing it with respect to student curricular expectations. Only through data analysis can staff determine normal and special variations in academic achievement and make changes to improve the program. Assessment is necessary to determine whether the academic program is enabling students to meet their expectations. Assessment is helpful to determine whether the sequence and scope is effective and any adjustments are needed. Assessment, analysis, and improvement of the curriculum must be never ending in order to continually improve student academic programs and achievements.

The curriculum is the school! It represents the values of the people. It speaks to the community and reflects its heart. It is what we stand for and wish to pass on through our children. The curriculum is "We the People!" (See figure 2.2.)

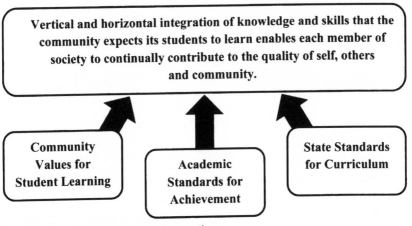

Figure 2.2. Curriculum-System Integration

VARIABLE-STRATEGIES INSTRUCTIONAL SYSTEM

The *instructional system* is the method by which the curriculum system is taught to the students. It is the method of instruction that the professional staff use to educate their students. Instructional strategies integrate many different content areas to enhance a student's ability to understand based on a series of different approaches to learning. Along with integrating ideas, the instructional strategies are designed to take on many forms and are sensitive to different learning styles within the student population.

Professional staff create an environment inviting and encouraging students to learn. Teachers organize experiences to clarify student expectations and challenge the cognitive abilities of each student. Along with levels of cognitive challenges, the teacher creates different learning activities that are sensitive to modes of learning and learning preferences and allows for each student to gain new knowledge in an appropriate manner.

It is through the instructional methods and processes that the art of teaching comes alive. Teacher skills and talents are pushed to their limits to meet this challenge. The joy of teaching is experienced when results are seen in the faces of the students who are learning. Teachers facilitate student thinking at all cognitive levels—knowledge, comprehension, application, analysis, evaluation, and synthesis.

Also, teachers use different modes of instruction such as large-group, small-group, lecture, individual, and collaborative study. The teacher's instructional design integrates different learning styles, such as sequential and random, along with abstract- and concrete-learning preferences.

Teachers create and implement these instructional methods and processes to educate our children. This is their most valued function and most creative act. The curriculum comes alive through the instructional methods, and student learning and achievement are the result! (See figure 2.3.)

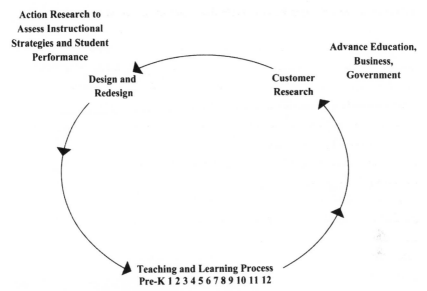

Figure 2.3. *Instructional System*

STATISTICALLY BASED ASSESSMENT SYSTEM

The *assessment system* is the evaluation of the instructional system and student academic-performance system. Through the assessment system, professional staff are able to gather and analyze data to determine the effectiveness of the instructional process and student academic performance. This analysis is essential to the continual improvement of the instructional system and student academic achievement.

After student-curriculum expectations are clarified, specific observable indicators are identified under each of the expectations. Assessment strategies are created to determine student achievement on each of the observable indicators, and data are gathered. These data are analyzed using statistical strategies, and professional staff determine trends in the data. As normal and special causes of variation are determined, staff can implement changes in the instructional system to improve the student academic program.

Instructional methods and student-performance results are analyzed to assure continual improvement of both instruction and achievement. It is through this assessment that the academic program is evaluated. Also, professional staff and community members can be assured that the education given to the students is meeting expectations. Assessment information is shared with school staff, and work teams made up of staff and community members suggest improvements for the academic program.

After these recommendations for academic-program improvement are received, reviewed, analyzed, and evaluated by the school academic-planning team, the team makes recommendations for future school improvement. Assessment of academic-program data in its various forms is the method of accountability that communities are looking for to assure academic quality.

As partnerships are created between professional staff and community members to share and understand academic-program expectations and results, opportunities for collaboration and cooperation to build better learning options for everyone can result. Everyone in the community needs to be valued as each person works to build a better learning environment for each student

A network consists of integrated systems, and each system consists of layers within itself. An example of a network with multiple systems and layers within each is given in the following section. An effective school leader integrates these five systems to create an effective network to achieve the aim of the total academic system, which is student achievement. (See figure 2.4.)

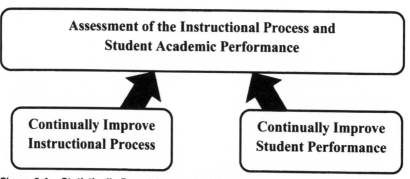

Figure 2.4.   Statistically Based Assessment Systems

NETWORK OF SYSTEMS AND LAYERS WITHIN EACH SYSTEM TO BE INTEGRATED

School organizational structure

Principal
Administrative team
Building-leadership team

Communication system integrating levels of inclusion

Teacher to teacher
Teacher teams
Teacher teams with planning time
Leadership team, teacher teams with planning time
Leadership team, teacher teams with planning time and minutes of meetings
District-leadership team, building-leadership team, teacher teams with planning time and minutes of meetings

Curriculum system integrating levels of depth

Curricular expectations
Curricular expectations and criteria
Curricular expectations, criteria, and observable indicators

Instructional system integrating levels of communication

Teacher and student
Instructional team, teacher, and student
Staff-development program, instructional team, teacher, and student
Parents, staff-development program, instructional team, teacher, and student

Statistically based assessment system integrating expectations

Criterion reference–assessment data gathering
Team data analysis using statistical control charts and item analysis
Recommendations of process designs for instructional improvement
Professional development for staff designed based on recommendations

VISIBLE LEARNING: A SYNTHESIS OF OVER META-ANALYSES RELATING TO ACHIEVEMENT

This meta-analysis relating to achievement challenges educators to address current instructional strategies, structural designs for learning, relationships with teachers, data supporting current practices, and implementing proven best practices in reading and writing. As one reviews the analysis of this study, the need for a collaborative integration of administrators, teachers, students, and parents is essential to bring about the continual improvement of the schooling process. Future educational systems must address flexibility and variability in the instructional options for students and the continual improvement philosophy is the foundation for building this new way of thinking.

> Independent of normal student ability, it takes three or four experiences involving interaction with relevant information for a new knowledge construct to be created in working memory and then transferred to long term memory. Numerous interactions mean not just repeating information but distributing the knowledge and "application in context" over a number of days. Students who have difficulty participating in a learning activity not only fail to acquire the knowledge they need to understand and acquire further knowledge; they learn that their ability to acquire knowledge is inferior. (Hattie 2009, 242)

Constructivism is a form of knowing and not a form of teaching, and it is important not to confuse constructing conceptual knowledge with the current fad of constructivism. Constructing conceptual knowledge involves considering learning from the learner's viewpoint, starting from the premise that all learners are active, appreciating that what they learn is socially constructed, and understanding that learners need to create and re-create knowledge of them. If this is the meaning of constructivism from a learner's perspective, then the more direct and active methods of teaching appear to be optimal for achieving this type of learning. The only way constructive thinking applies to teaching is to the teachers themselves, as they construct concepts, beliefs, and models about how they teach and how students learn. The methods that work best, as identified from the synthesis of the meta-analyses, lead to a very active, direct involvement, and high sense of urgency, in the learning and teaching process. Such teaching leads to higher levels of learning, autonomy, and self-regulation on behalf of the learners, whether they are students or teachers. (Hattie 2009, 243)

It is sobering to realize that we have a teaching cohort that is average, at best, in the eyes of most students. It is sobering to realize that each child will meet only a few teachers [whom] they will consider to have a lasting and positive effect on them. It is sobering to realize that these teachers will be remembered not because they taught social studies or mathematics but because they cared about teaching the students their passion for their subject, gave students confidence in themselves as learners and as people, treated the student as a person, and instilled a love of learning of their subjects. (Hattie 2009, 250)

After reviewing over five thousand student cases referred to school psychologists because the students were failing in school, not one case located the problem as due to an instructional program, poor school practices, a poor teacher, or something to do with school. The problems were claimed, by the teachers, to be related to the home and located within the student. "An arrogant system would conclude that all the problems were caused by defects in the children, none caused by any defect in the school system." The researchers challenge teachers and schools to ask with respect to what the teachers and school are implementing:

1. Precisely where have you seen this practice installed so that it produces effective results?
2. Precisely where have you trained teachers so they can uniformly perform within the guidelines of this new system?
3. Where is the data that shows you have achieved performance that is superior to that achieved by successful programs in place at this time?
4. Where are the endorsements from historically successful teachers?

The depressing news is that "the closer an innovation gets to the core of schooling, the less likely it is that it will influence teaching and learning on a large scale," and reciprocally those further away from teaching and learning are more likely to become national policies. The problem is not general resistance or failure of schools to change as schools are constantly changing. The resistance is with the conceptions of teaching and learning shared by teachers. We in education place most of the problems for a lack of student learning not on the teachers or the schools. Also, it is almost impossible to legislate changes to concepts of teaching and learning, and this is where professional development becomes critical. So often the policy changes have little or no effect on conceptions of teaching and learning. (Hattie 2009, 253)

We spend millions of dollars investing in innovations, changes, and policies in education without a lot of evidence that this investment is making a difference to student outcomes. They make a major difference to teachers' and students' working conditions but not to the achievement outcomes. Does the innovation meet the (average d = .40) growth expectation that indicates significant improvement? (Hattie 2009, 255)

Changing teachers' conceptions is not easy or cheap. Teachers will not just move from not doing a new behavior to doing it. They go through decision phases: awareness, knowledge, persuasion, confusion, decision, implementation, and confirmation. In analyzing the study of teaching over the past two hundred years, 85 percent of teachers are resistant to change what works for them, 10 percent are willing to change to be more efficient, and 5 percent are willing to try new innovations. (Hattie 2009, 257)

Some findings after studying effective elementary teachers, especially those effective in the areas of reading and writing, are that they

1. devote much of the class time to academic activities that require students to think as they read, write and discuss materials
2. teach and reteach skills through modeling and explaining skills followed by guided practice
3. show a strong balance between instructional skills and holistic reading and writing activities
4. scaffold and [reteach] knowledge and skills
5. integrate content knowledge learning to reading and writing instruction
6. [and] have high expectations and increase academic demands on their students. (Hattie 2009, 261)

REFLECTIONS

Reflecting on the issues addressed by John Hattie, as well as the ongoing development of new knowledge and technology, every leader must understand systems, variations within systems, and the integrations of systems to meet the future demands of our students. The systems introduced in this chapter and their implementations into our nation's schools are essential to our future. Our educational system must educate students who are capable of higher-level thinking, identifying problems and creating solutions to lead our country into the future.

SCHOOL-SYSTEM EVALUATION SURVEY

This survey consists of fifty items (the complete survey is in appendix A). It is recommended that you take the entire survey before continuing your study of this material. Then, after you study chapters 2 through 6, assess the system addressed at the end of each of these chapters. Compare your perceptions of the data from the pre- and postassessment. There are ten items to assess in this chapter and ten items in each of the next four chapters. You are asked to determine whether or not each item is present in your working environment. Also, it is very important that you not judge each item as good or bad, desirable or undesirable, but that you determine to what degree the item is present in your work environment. The range of choices is 1 through 9—1 indicating never present and 9 indicating always present. (See figure 2.5.)

Please indicate the number that reflects your perception of each item present in your work environment at this time. Assess your professional staff as to their understanding and implementation of these ten best practices of key elements of a system.

Never   About Half   Always

1   2   3   4   5   6   7   8   9

Figure 2.5.

1. School Academic-System Structures and Elements

    1.1 *Professional staff understands the concept of* system. A *system* is defined as a series of components that work together within an organization for the purpose (*aim*) of the organization. Each component in a system works together to benefit other components in a system and to achieve the aim of the total system. (In the organizational system, components such as time schedule, instructional teams, team planning time, curriculum design, and classroom organization are key components.) Three key elements in understanding a system are defining the system, clarifying the purpose of the system, and determining by what method the purpose will be achieved in the system.

         1   2   3   4   5   6   7   8   9

    1.2 *Professional staff identifies key system components.* Each major system component and its function are identified. (One component of the school organizational system is the *communication structure and process* for decision making.) Without identification, the component and its relationship to other components are not clear and the system is not effective.

         1   2   3   4   5   6   7   8   9

    1.3 *Professional staff state system purposes.* The system purpose or aim gives meaning to the integration of all components. If the purpose or aim of the system is not stated clearly, each component cannot perform its function as it serves the system.

         1   2   3   4   5   6   7   8   9

1.4   *Professional staff clarify system purposes.* Once the system purpose or aim is stated, the words need to be clarified or defined so everyone understands the statement. Everyone working on the system has to have the same understanding of the purpose of the system.

      1   2   3   4   5   6   7   8   9

1.5   *Professional staff communicate system purposes.* Once the system purpose or aim is stated and clarified, the purpose or aim is communicated in writing to all partners within the system. The purpose is clearly stated so all members working on the system maintain a clear and constant focus.

      1   2   3   4   5   6   7   8   9

1.6   *Professional staff identify methods to achieve system purposes. Methods* are the means by which the purpose of the system is achieved. Instructional strategies, for example, are the methods teachers use to achieve the purpose of student learning.

      1   2   3   4   5   6   7   8   9

1.7   *Professional staff assess system purposes.* Gathering data on specific purpose indicators is the means by which the system is assessed. Without gathering data on key elements of the system, staff are not able to evaluate the system with respect to process improvement and system results. If a specific system strategy is implemented, data on this strategy as well as system performance using this strategy need to be gathered.

      1   2   3   4   5   6   7   8   9

1.8   *Professional staff statistically analyze system data.* Data are gathered on system indicators (criteria) identified by the staff, such as effective decision making, team collaboration, and statistical data analysis. System statistical analysis is used to identify data trends and causes of variation.

      1   2   3   4   5   6   7   8   9

1.9   *Professional staff identify trends based on the data.* The staff recognize academic trends based on the data analysis. These trends are discussed with respect to implications for improvement.

1   2   3   4   5   6   7   8   9

1.10   *Professional staff implement improvement strategies.* The staff implement revised strategies based on the academic organizational-improvement trends supported by the data analysis. Improvement is judged on moving the system population in the direction of the system purpose or aim.

1   2   3   4   5   6   7   8   9

NOTE

1. And see *Wikipedia.org*, n.d., s.v. "Project Lead the Way," http://en.wikipedia.org/wiki/Project_Lead_The_Way (accessed February 11, 2014).

CHAPTER 3

Communication System

> *System*: Communication
> *System aim*: Effective decisions to improve the academic program
> *Methodology*: Integrated linkage of all communication levels

As was mentioned in the previous chapter, there are many structural variations in the organizational patterns of our schools across the nation. Each structure has its own communication system or lack thereof. The aim in this chapter is to share the continual-improvement philosophy through cooperation and collaboration in the design of a linked communication system that respects and values each member of the professional staff.

This is based on the belief that nothing can be accomplished by the professional staff unless a well-linked communication system is designed and implemented using people-process integration skills to make it function well. Communication is essential in any positive relationship. The purpose of the communication system is to inform people in order to make more effective decisions. In order to improve the curriculum, instruction, and assessment systems, the professional staff need an effective communication system.

The principal is in the position to implement this system and is responsible for collaborating with the professional staff to create this system. Professional-staff development must address the concept of *system thinking* and understand the notion of working on the system to improve it. Also, the concepts of everyone winning, shared values, and team support are difficult to understand unless everyone internalizes the notion that it is no longer acceptable to gain from someone else's loss.

The purpose of the *school-improvement planning process* is to enhance student learning. Everything the school staff do has this as its aim. Without an effective communication system, the staff decision-making process is impeded from achieving its purpose. An effective communication system is to the school as an effective circulatory system is to the body. If this system does not flow properly, confusion and doubt negatively impact the system and cause it to malfunction. Any system cannot survive without an open ongoing effective and efficient two-way flow of communication.

The criterion for decision making within the communication system is to determine the appropriate level at which action must be taken. If the decision affects only the level at which it is being implemented, the decision is made at that level. If the issue being discussed has an impact beyond the level at which it is being discussed, it must move to the agenda at the next level up in the organization. The four levels addressed in this model are the instructional team, the building-leadership team, the district-leadership team, and the school board of education.

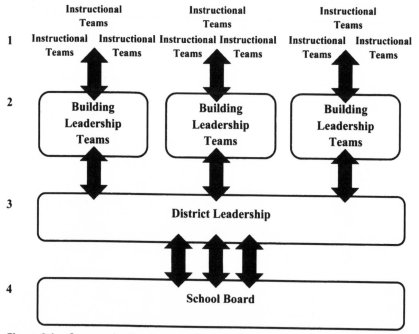

Figure 3.1.   Communication-Integrated Linkage Model

The communication system is structured to enable and enhance cooperation and collaboration to continually improve the academic functioning of the school. In order for the principal and faculty to make efficient and effective decisions, the communication system is designed to inform and invest everyone in the school in the communication process.

Linkage of levels within the communication system is important and allows for the transfer of information. The communication system links the school's internal operations to the district's operations so that the whole communication system operates to achieve the aim of continual improvement of the academic process. To achieve this aim, at least four levels of communication are necessary.

INSTRUCTIONAL TEAM

The *instructional team* makes up the first level of communication, which consists of the faculty—a team leader, other teachers, and other instructional staff at a particular grade level, across grade levels, within a subject area or across subject areas. It is important to structure the daily school schedule so that the instructional teams have planning time during the school day. This is the time the teachers use for instructional planning, school-related problem solving, student-data analysis, content analysis, school-improvement planning, and many other related issues.

The instructional team has specific roles, responsibilities, and attributes. Namely, the instructional team

1. is represented by a teacher leader elected by the team
2. meets during the specified planning time within the school day
3. records minutes of issues discussed and team decisions
4. shares its decisions with the building-level team
5. participates in the school-improvement planning process
6. implements district philosophy and instructional beliefs
7. implements the school-improvement plan
8. implements the district curriculum
9. assesses student academic performance

10. analyzes student-performance data
11. analyzes instructional strategies
12. coordinates instructional strategies
13. designs instructional units of study
14. determines student instructional grouping
15. recommends curriculum improvement
16. recommends instructional improvement
17. recommends an instructional-materials budget
18. and, finally, recommends future staff-development issues.

The instructional-team leader has specific roles, responsibilities, and attributes. Namely, the instructional-team leader

1. coordinates team activities
2. clarifies instructional needs
3. supports team instructional strategies
4. supports instructional-improvement strategies
5. coordinates instructional research and data analysis
6. participates on the building-instructional-improvement committee
7. facilitates curriculum alignment
8. communicates information between the team and the building committee
9. and, finally, conducts instructional-team meetings.

BUILDING-LEADERSHIP TEAM

The second level of communication is the building-leadership team. This level consists of the principal and the team leaders from the instructional teams. This team meets once a week to address agenda items submitted by the principal and faculty. The decisions made at this meeting are recorded and distributed to the building staff for further discussion at the instructional-team meetings. This two-way communication process allows for issues to be discussed and decided with total knowledge and participation by all staff in the school.

The building-leadership team has specific roles and responsibilities. Namely, the building-leadership team

1. is chaired by the principal
2. meets weekly
3. sets the agenda one day prior to meeting
4. records and sends minutes to all building staff after the day following the meeting
5. coordinates processes for student, parent, and community involvement
6. coordinates the school-improvement planning process
7. coordinates the academic-assessment plan
8. coordinates curriculum alignment
9. analyzes academic data
10. shares the academic data with school staff
11. monitors instructional strategies
12. writes the school-improvement plan
13. determines the school schedule
14. determines the building staff's academic needs
15. determines the building staff's development program
16. determines the building's instructional-space usage
17. schedules team-planning time
18. recommends the instructional budget
19. recommends instructional improvement
20. recommends curriculum improvement
21. and, finally, recommends issues for the district-leadership team.

The principal has certain roles, responsibilities, and attributes. Namely the principal

1. leads instructional improvement through organizing instructional teams
2. works with the teams, team members, and team leaders
3. chairs the building instructional-improvement leadership team
4. facilitates the in-service for instructional improvement
5. facilitates curriculum implementation

6. facilitates instructional research and data analysis
7. supports the instructional program
8. supervises and evaluates the staff and instructional program
9. and, finally, supports changes to improve the academic programs.

DISTRICT-LEADERSHIP COUNCIL

At the third level of communication is the district-leadership council, which includes the superintendent and/or associate superintendent of curriculum and instruction, school board representatives, and principals and/or team leaders from each of the schools in the district. The principal and team-leader representatives should be evenly split among the representative schools in the district. Each school is represented at this level and addresses district-level issues.

The district-leadership council has specific roles, responsibilities, and attributes. Namely, the district-leadership council

1. is chaired by the superintendent or associate superintendent
2. meets monthly
3. sets the agenda five days prior to the meeting
4. records and sends minutes to all members and schools
5. implements processes for student, parent, and community involvement
6. monitors district academic programs
7. monitors district assessment programs
8. facilitates communications among schools
9. plans and implements district professional development
10. recommends the district's curriculum program
11. recommends district instructional materials
12. recommends the district's assessment program
13. and, finally, recommends issues to the school board for discussion.

DISTRICT SCHOOL BOARD OF EDUCATION

The fourth level of communication is the district school board of education. The role of the school board is to initiate and implement school policies that optimize the continual improvement of student academic programs and school operations.

The school board of education has specific roles, responsibilities, and attributes. Namely, the school board of education

1. assesses the recommendations from the district instructional-improvement council
2. approves the recommendations supportive of the continual-improvement process
3. supports professional development of the administrative and teaching staff
4. supports research on the instructional system
5. communicates and supports the aims of the district
6. communicates the values and priorities of the district community
7. budgets for continual improvement of the instructional system
8. and, finally, reviews each school-improvement plan.

Once this communication system is in place, one of the first functions of the building-leadership team is to use this system to create the *school academic-improvement plan*, which has many stages and involves many people. It starts with the faculty being involved in determining the student academic performance at each level in the school.

Once the data are gathered and analyzed, academic priorities are determined and improvement strategies suggested. This is a time-consuming process and depends on an effective communication system. The principal is the key to the success of this process because it is the principal who includes the faculty and members of the community in the planning process. The leadership determines the effectiveness of this system.

SCHOOL ACADEMIC-PLANNING PROCESS

The professional staff review student academic data and decide the priorities to be addressed in the following academic year. Student academic-performance data are analyzed, after which the instructional teams make recommendations to the building instructional-improvement team. The building instructional-improvement team recommends the final school-improvement priorities for the following academic year. The building-leadership team discusses the recommendations with the community representatives from the school community and addresses their concerns, then revising the recommendations for the final school-improvement plan.

The building instructional-improvement team has certain roles, responsibilities, and attributes. Namely, the building-instructional team

1. reviews student-performance data
2. analyzes student-performance data
3. recommends academic priorities to the building level
4. reviews academic priorities
5. shares these priorities with the other critical groups
6. decides on final school-improvement priorities
7. drafts the school-improvement plan
8. shares the plan with the instructional teams to collect feedback
9. and, finally, writes the final school-improvement plan.

The principal involves the faculty in the writing of the *academic-improvement plan*. The writing of this plan is the method by which the faculty take ownership of the continual improvement of the academic program and school-improvement plan priorities. The principal leads the faculty through a group process where the school clarifies vision and purpose. Then the faculty clarify the student-academic expectations at each grade level. Later in the school year, student-achievement and instructional-process data are collected and analyzed, which allows for a review of future academic priorities and instructional strategies for improvement.

The principal is the key person who leads the faculty through this process. No one else can do it. No one else *should* do it! The principal is the instructional leader of the school and must lead the staff in these important responsibilities. In the future, we will see more states requiring *academic-improvement plans* and requiring school-improvement planning processes. It is a positive way to go, and an effective leader values and welcomes this process.

The school-improvement plan consists of the following sections:

1.0   Academic philosophy (mission and beliefs)
2.0   Academic aims (purpose and objectives)
3.0   Academic-data analysis (local and national assessments)
4.0   Academic priorities (curriculum trends and data analysis)
5.0   Improvement strategies (improvement summary)
6.0   Assessment of strategies (performance summary)
7.0   Community update (communication plan)

The principal coordinates the writing of the school-improvement planning process.

1.0   Instructional teams review student-performance data.
2.0   Instructional teams analyze student-performance data.
3.0   Instructional teams recommend academic priorities to the building level.
4.0   The building team reviews academic priorities.
5.0   The building team shares these priorities with the other community groups.
6.0   The building team decides on the final school-improvement priorities.
7.0   The building team drafts the school-improvement plan.
8.0   The plan is shared with the instructional teams to garner feedback.
9.0   The building team writes the final school-improvement plan.

In order to enhance the effectiveness of the communication system, building administrative leaders must organize the faculty into instructional teams. Teams can be organized by grade level, multigrade level, integrated academic grade level, or multigrade integrated-academic grade level. Examples of these structures might be first-grade teams; first-, second-, and third-grade teams; middle-school integrated-academic area teams; high school math teams; and so on.

The faculty must understand that information needs to be discussed within instructional teams and that suggestions for improvement come from this knowledge base. The more the building administrative leaders can involve the faculty in the decision-making process, the better the ownership and implementation of ideas will occur. Administrative leaders must value instructional teams to give support to the faculty and build collaboration.

The district administrative staff meet with the principals and professional staffs to discuss the organizational structures that might be implemented in the schools to enhance instruction. After the organizational structures are decided, the building leaders, along with the professional staff, organize the teachers into instructional teams consistent with the academic aims of the school. The organizational structure can vary from grade-level teams to multigrade-level teams, multiage teams, content-area teams, integrated content–area teams, or any other structure that achieves the academic aim of the school.

COMMON PLANNING TIME

The key is to have the organizational structure support the academic program and the decision-making process at the instructional and building-team levels throughout the schools. One issue that is essential in the design process is to assure planning time for each instructional team within each school day. This time is essential for the instructional teams to succeed in carrying out their responsibilities. Without common planning time for the instructional teams, the value of collaboration is defeated.

The spirit of the faculty is supported through the work of these instructional teams. It is in the common planning time that the work of the instructional program is achieved. It is the common planning time that enables the instructional team to create integrated units of study, discuss school-related issues, determine budget allocations for instructional supplies, discuss student priorities, analyze data, and suggest improvement strategies and many other critical issues.

Common planning times for the instructional teams are the most telling evidence of valuing the faculty as professional teachers. The instructional team needs to be free from students during common team-planning time for it to be effective. Students might travel to other

ACADEMIC BLOCK SCHEDULE FOR INSTRUCTIONAL TEAM PLANNING

	BLOCK 1	BLOCK 2	BLOCK 3	BLOCK 4	BLOCK 5
TEAM A	CLASS	CLASS	CLASS	CLASS	**PLAN**
TEAM B	CLASS	CLASS	CLASS	**PLAN**	CLASS
TEAM C	CLASS	CLASS	**PLAN**	CLASS	CLASS
TEAM D	CLASS	**PLAN**	CLASS	CLASS	CLASS
TEAM E	**PLAN**	CLASS	CLASS	CLASS	CLASS

Figure 3.2.   Academic-Block Schedule

academic areas to free up an instructional team. The principal is responsible for creating this plan but need not do it alone. Many faculty members are willing to work with the principal to create this plan and work out the details for all to benefit.

If block scheduling is used to create common planning time for the instructional teams, instructional blocks of time need to equal the number of teams within the instructional time schedule (see figure 3.2). This allows for instructional-planning time for each team during the school day. As the students move from block to block, planning time becomes available while the students go to a different block of academic subjects—such as special areas, interest-group classes, advisory sessions, and so on. The common planning time for instructional teams is the backbone of the instructional-improvement system. Also, this is the time to discuss building-level issues, such as instructional-space usage and academic priorities.

CONSENSUS PROCESS

One of the process skills the teams needs to implement is a consensus method for decision making. *Consensus* is defined as supporting a decision even if one does not agree with it totally. The key is not to undermine the decision and harm the chances of its having a chance to succeed. The reason consensus is essential in certain situations is that voting does not always work and minority resentment can destroy the attitude of the faculty over time.

An example of where voting is not effective is in the budget-allocation process. The areas of fine arts and physical education, for example, may be outvoted on needs for their programs if only voting is used. Other areas may suffer also, such as the media center and the after-school programs. The principal and instructional-team leaders at the building level are the people who can use good judgment to determine which issues need consensus for final decision making.

The principal is responsible for assuring professional-staff development in this area, and the faculty must understand this process of decision making. This process is used at the instructional-team level as well as the building level for critical decisions. It is true that decisions may take more time under this process, but the long-term gain is well worth it. Many times consensus is negotiated among the staff to help each other try different ideas to find out whether or not they work. Sometimes a pilot program is agreed upon, and the staff supports it just to see if it works.

The budget process is one area where the consensus process is mandatory. If it is not used, some areas in the academic program may be ignored or inadequately funded. The continual-improvement philosophy requires that everyone benefit and that no one take advantage of others. The budget process is where this method is of utmost importance.

CONSENSUS METHOD

At each level of the communication system, many decisions might be best decided by consensus. Often, voting does not meet the concerns of a minority position and if, in this case, a decision is voted upon resentment can result from a lack of understanding of the minority concern. If this happens too often, the climate of the sensitivity within the leadership team can become negative. Again, *consensus* is the willingness to go along with the decision and support the decision even if one does not agree with it totally.

One method many groups use to assess and analyze consensus is the *finger: 1-3-5* method. The leader asks the group to show where they are on an issue. Each person is asked to indicate their level of support for the issue by placing a hand on the table in the following manner: A hand showing all five fingers indicates total support for the idea. Three fingers show positive support with minor concerns. One finger shows lack of support and a wish for further discussion of the idea. This process can be used to assess support as the team moves toward consensus.

AGENDA PROCESS

Agendas are created for the meeting of the building-leadership team, which consists of the principal and the instructional-team leaders. The items for the agenda are to be in the principal's office two days before the meeting. This time line allows the agenda to be sent to each instructional team for dialogue before the building-leadership team meeting. The leadership team discusses the items on the agenda, and the results of the discussion are recorded in the minutes. No item can be added at the meeting and nothing discussed that is not on the agenda. If issues on the agenda are in need of other input, people can be invited to the meeting to add information. All building-leadership meetings are open to the staff and the community at all times.

1. Agenda items are written and shared with the instructional teams in advance of the building-leadership meeting to allow team discussion on the items.
2. Agenda items are submitted by the instructional teams.
3. Agenda items are submitted by the principal.
4. No agenda item can be added after the agenda is sent to the instructional teams.
5. No items are addressed at the leadership meeting if they are not already on the agenda.

The principal meets with the instructional-team leaders once a week to address school issues. The instructional-team leader shares the various team teachers' views on issues and votes on issues at the building-level meeting when needed. It is important that a team leader not state only his or her personal view on any issue or ignore the team members' views on any issue in the discussion at the building-leadership team meeting. All parties' views on any issue must be shared and considered at the building-level meeting.

The instructional team–leader position may change each year, and it is recommended that no additional release time or pay be given for this responsibility. If any advantage of release time or pay is given to this role, other team members may feel all the team members are not equal in the team's responsibilities, and it may negatively affect team effectiveness. The instructional-team leader is the communication link between the instructional team and the building-leadership team.

The principal- and instructional-team leaders meet weekly to address the agenda items submitted by the teams and principal. The meeting is scheduled to take place after school hours have ended to allow all team leaders to attend. The meeting may last about an hour and is focused on the agenda. The principal needs to go through each item at the start of the meeting and share the type of decision needed on the item. Once information items are addressed, the team's work begins on the items needing discussion and decisions.

MEETING MINUTES

The minutes taken at the building-leadership meeting are reviewed by the principal and are written and given to each professional staff member the next morning after the building-leadership team meeting. The team leader is responsible for discussing and clarifying the minutes with the team members at the next day's common planning-time meeting. Many times the minutes may not be clearly written or perhaps team members may misunderstand the intent of the decisions.

The follow-up discussion by the team leader allows for clarification and proper understanding of the issues stated in the minutes of the building-level meeting. This accurate flow of information is critical to the effectiveness of the communication system. The instructional teams review and discuss the building-leadership team minutes and determine how to implement any decisions agreed upon in the leadership-team meeting. If there is additional information needed on other items, the team leader addresses this, and then the team moves on to other team matters.

It is important that the team members understand and discuss the decisions with respect to the agenda items so everyone is informed on the issues important to the school community. Informed faculty are the strength of the continual-improvement system, and the communication system is the lifeline of the process. The principal and the team leaders keep copies of the building-leadership team meetings for a record of the building history. Many times an issue returns, and so it is helpful to have past records to review the issue. Also, these documents help new staff members understand the history of an issue and not make mistakes because of a lack of knowledge.

COMMUNICATION-SYSTEM SURVEY

2.0   Communication System

    2.1   *Professional staff respect the philosophy of continual improvement through their cooperative efforts to achieve academic improvement.* This philosophy enables staff members to work together for their mutual benefit and the improvement of the academic program. In order to cooperate, staff are sufficiently aware of relevant information on issues so as to make informed decisions. Cooperation is demonstrated through mutual trust and respect for all parties to gain and for no party to gain at the expense of another. Staff work within an academic system, leaders work on the academic system, and everyone works toward continual improvement of the academic system to achieve the purpose of student learning.

        1   2   3   4   5   6   7   8   9

    2.2   *Professional staff participate in the school academic-improvement planning process.* Staff are informed of the student-performance data at each grade or course level in the school. Based on the data analysis, staff recommend curricular priorities and suggest strategies for improvement to be stated in the academic school-improvement plan.

        1   2   3   4   5   6   7   8   9

2.3   *Professional staff and others write the academic school-improvement plan.* Staff work together to write the academic school-improvement plan:

1.0   Academic philosophy (mission and beliefs)
2.0   Academic aims (purpose and objectives)
3.0   Academic-data analysis (local and national assessments)
4.0   Academic priorities (curriculum trends and analysis)
5.0   Improvement strategies (improvement summary)
6.0   Assessment of strategies (performance summary)
7.0   Community update (communication plan)

1   2   3   4   5   6   7   8   9

2.4   *Administrator organizes staff into instructional teams.* These teams are determined by grade-level (first grade), multidiscipline (sixth-grade content areas), multigrade level (first, second, third grade), or content area (high school math). These instructional teams are organized to integrate content and methodology to enhance student learning.

1   2   3   4   5   6   7   8   9

2.5   *Administrator schedules common planning time during the school day for instructional teams.* Instructional teams have common planning time for professional collaboration. This time is used for planning curricular units, designing instructional strategies, designing assessment methods, and continually improving the academic system.

1   2   3   4   5   6   7   8   9

2.6   *Instructional teams use consensus methods to make decisions.* Consensus decision making is defined as each person accepting the decision. Agreement with the decision is not critical; however, willingness to go along with the decision *is* critical. If a person is not able to come to this level of acceptance, the discussion must continue until consensus is reached.

1   2   3   4   5   6   7   8   9

2.7   *Administrators and teachers create an agenda for the building-leadership team meetings.* The administrators and teachers create an agenda. The agenda is written and shared with the instructional teams prior to the meeting, and no item is added to the agenda after it is shared with the instructional teams. If new agenda items are identified after the agenda has gone out, the new items go on the next agenda.

1   2   3   4   5   6   7   8   9

2.8   *Administrator meets with instructional-team leaders weekly to address academic improvement.* Instructional-team leaders represent the instructional team. These representatives meet with an administrator weekly to discuss various issues for improvement with respect to academic organization, communication, curriculum, instruction, and assessment improvements.

1   2   3   4   5   6   7   8   9

2.9   *Instructional teams receive written minutes of the building-team leadership meetings.* Written minutes are shared with each staff member the next day. The minutes contain each agenda item, the decision, and the rationale.

1   2   3   4   5   6   7   8   9

2.10 *Instructional-team leaders review building-leadership meeting minutes with team members.* Team leaders clarify and discuss the building-leadership meeting minutes with team members.

1   2   3   4   5   6   7   8   9

CHAPTER 4

Curriculum System

System: Curriculum

System aim: Teach students our values and standards

Methodology: *Traditional curriculum design*: Determine values, concepts, and standards; align, integrate, and sequence scope and depth of curriculum and criteria for assessment of learning outcomes

Content-integrated curriculum design: Determine values, concepts, and standards; some content areas that are integrated (math and science, history and language arts, art and music, or multiple integrations of various content areas); independent courses; courses somewhat topic aligned; separate course assessment; and some common assignments

Thematic integrated-unit curriculum design: Determine values, concepts, and standards; themes for units; unit outcomes; learning stations; scope and depth within the unit; and criteria for learning outcomes

Project based–learning curriculum design: Determine values, concepts, and standards; select projects; and identify project process steps and time lines, project outcome expectations, and assessment criteria for learning outcomes

Problem based–learning curriculum design: Determine values, concepts, and standards; select problems to be solved; identify student problem-solving process steps and expectations, and assessment criteria and time lines

Independent curriculum design: Determine values, concepts, and standards; student selects concepts, content, units, projects, and problems; student selects appropriate process steps for each model of study; student creates assessment criteria; and student evaluates and presents final reports

PERSONAL STORY

Today there are as many variations in curricular design as there are publishers in our nation. Any professional staff member is hard pressed to determine a curricular program that meets all their needs and addresses all of their student priorities with respect to content, design, and delivery. I recall that when I was a new middle-school principal the professional staff were not pleased with the reading results of our students and were very frustrated with the reading program.

The staff were using a single publisher program and did not think it was flexible enough to address the students' variations in reading levels at each grade level. It lacked both materials for different learning styles and various teaching activities, and it had limited assessment strategies. All in all, the program was not acceptable to meet the academic needs of the students and staff. However, the school district was not in the financial position to make any major changes at the time.

Upon further investigation, some professional staff found that many other reading materials from multiple publishers were stored in closets and on shelves throughout the building. This information was presented to the entire staff, and a challenge was offered to them: Since many of the staff had excellent academic and practical-reading backgrounds, they could choose to design and implement a new reading program that would meet student needs using all the existing publisher materials.

The professional staff accepted the challenge and spent half of that academic year designing the reading curriculum, selecting appropriate teaching materials, and designing assessment strategies using all the different reading materials available with no additional cost to the district.

To begin, the first step was for the staff to assess each child's individual reading-inventory level and actual needs—and not rely on a standardized reading-test score to analyze an individual student-reading need. These data were the greatest eye opener to the staff. The results of the student-reading inventory assessments are shown in figure 4.1 (Warwick 1995, chap. 3).

Even the most experienced teacher had no idea of the student variation in these scores and was determined to design a new reading program. The real shocker was when the reading-specialist teacher shared with the faculty that the score on the inventory was not the reading level

Grade Level	Grade Level Equivalent										
	3	4	5	6	7	8	9	10	11	12	Total
5	4	11	22	31	28	15	7	8			126
6	1	2	11	26	21	15	18	11	7	4	116
7	2	1	0	15	11	24	13	12	16	11	105
8	0	2	3	3	11	16	17	13	8	21	94
Total	7	16	36	75	71	70	55	44	31	36	441

Figure 4.1. **Twin Grove Middle School Student-Reading Inventory Data**

of the student but the student's reading-frustration score. She went on to explain that the frustration score is one score higher than the reading level of the student. A student who scores a grade-equivalency score of 7, for example, is reading at level 6. This was news to all the staff!

The next thing was to change the school schedule to have a one and a half hour block of time in the morning just for reading. This time was to be used for reading-skills groups, group reading, and silent reading. Reading-skills groups were scheduled by reading-level equivalency throughout the school. Skill groups were limited to three grade levels at most because of parent concerns. The staff spent the second half of the school year implementing this program and addressing the student reading needs for the first time based on accurate data. As a result, the students made the highest gains in their reading scores at the end of this school year in the history of the school. The continual-improvement process started with the reading program, and this process had an impact on all the other areas of the curriculum as time passed.

CURRICULUM-DESIGN SYSTEMS: TRADITIONAL, CONTENT INTEGRATED, THEMATIC INTEGRATED, PROJECT BASED, PROBLEM BASED, AND INDEPENDENT STUDY

Of the various curriculum-design options listed above, some of the variables to consider are

1. teacher instruction, selection of content, learning strategies, assessment methods

2. student instruction, selection of content, learning strategies, assessment methods
3. student's opportunity to develop problem-solving and decision-making skills
4. student's opportunity to develop and implement collaborative skills
5. and student's opportunity to assess and reflect on learning experiences and performance.

Also, as the professional staff assess the needs of the student body they serve, variations in student capacities—such as social awareness, cultural diversity, emotional development, intellectual development, physical development, and many other variables—are to be considered in the curriculum design.

The continuum from traditional to independent curriculum design moves from teacher control to student control in the various responsibilities for teaching and learning. There is no one design that is able to meet this range of student variation and flexibility in one curriculum system design. The challenge for every school district is to meet each student's academic and social-developmental needs with options in a flexibly designed curriculum system.

COMMON-CORE STATE STANDARDS AS THE BASES FOR CURRICULAR-DESIGN EXPECTATIONS

The principal and faculty are accountable for teaching the students in their care the curriculum expected by the school board and the state Department of Education. The misconception many educators have is that the *curriculum* and the *state standards* are the same thing. They are not! The *common-core state standards* are the minimum expectations the school should be addressing in the curriculum of the school. The curriculum should reflect common-core state standards, local community priorities, professional-organization best practices, and faculty content priorities.

The common-core standard curriculum is determined by each state's Department of Education. Each school district is accountable for teaching the state's standard curriculum, and the methods of instruction are determined by the professional staff in the school district. Many steps in designing how the curriculum is addressed are similar throughout many schools. However, each curriculum design must address critical-thinking skill levels as well as be sufficiently flexible to meet variations in student-learning processes.

COMMON CORE OF CRITICAL-THINKING LEVELS

Not only is the assessment of student knowledge of each content-area standard important, but the assessment of each cognitive level within that standard is also equally important. Each instructional system needs to be designed to address each level of thinking within the content covered in the curriculum. The cognitive levels addressed are *knowledge, comprehension, application, analysis, evaluation,* and *synthesis.*

Knowledge (remembering) is demonstrated through remembering facts and memorizing important information. This level of thinking does not require understanding the information that is remembered.

Comprehension (understanding) is demonstrated through explaining information and ideas in one's own words either by writing or telling the information.

Application (applying) is demonstrated through using learned information to solve a situation never experienced before and being able to address the issue.

Analysis (analysis) is demonstrated through identifying different aspects of a situation and explaining the relationship between and among the different elements in the situation.

Evaluation (evaluating) is demonstrated through assessing the acceptability or unacceptability of an event against known and previously agreed-upon criteria.

Synthesis (creating) is demonstrated through integrating individual elements that seem unrelated and creating a new outcome from these distinct elements. (Bloom 1956)

TRADITIONAL CURRICULUM DESIGN

Curriculum Alignment

As the faculty align the curriculum, knowledge of the students' readiness is essential in the design process. Once the student knowledge level is determined, student academic expectations are determined with respect to standards, community interests, best practices, and faculty knowledge. Once the curriculum alignment is determined, the sequence, scope, and depth of the curriculum can be determined.

It is clear why each school's curriculum is unique: The principal and faculty design the curriculum to meet the needs of the community it serves. Each community has different needs and interests that are reflected in the priorities of the curriculum program. The curriculum-alignment process enables faculty and community cooperation to determine the academic program.

As the professional staff align the curriculum to determine the sequence in which it is taught, the scope and depth can then be addressed. Through the process of curriculum alignment, the faculty comes to agreement on the academic expectations for each grade level and course and understands their relationship to previous and future academic expectations. As student academic expectations are clarified at each level by the appropriate faculty, the curricular system is identified and affirmed. Unless the faculty own the alignment process, the curriculum does not become clear and the vertical and horizontal integrations are not understood.

Even though most schools have curriculum guides for the grade-level subject areas and high school courses, many teachers are not clear on these student expectations in these academic areas if they have not been involved in reviewing and analyzing the curriculum. It is through this identification and affirmation process that the faculty develop ownership and commitment to the curriculum. If this faculty ownership does not occur, the curriculum system may not be implemented as intended. This lack of curriculum implementation may have a negative effect on all the other academic systems and the students.

As the faculty affirm the student academic expectations at a level of study, the depth of knowledge is clarified as well. The faculty understand that knowledge at one level must integrate with knowledge at the next level, and this laddering effect continues throughout the instructional process. As the faculty move through this process, the order and depth with which student academic expectations are addressed become matters of great concern. The age, ability, and capacity of the students are essential to the design of the curriculum. The concepts of vertical and horizontal integration, sequence, scope, and depth become essential as the faculty create the curriculum alignment.

The process steps for the school staff to achieve curriculum alignment are stated below. These steps are general in nature because the following two sections go into greater detail with respect to vertical and horizontal curriculum alignment. The steps that follow can be used to explain the process at a professional-staff meeting and in order for everyone to understand the big picture. These steps can be implemented in any content area and at any level.

1.0 Faculty members at each grade or course level write down on 5" × 8" index cards each curriculum expectation for the students at the content area and level desired based on common-core state standards, professional-content standards, best-practices research, and community expectations. (This step could be done electronically, and sorting and grouping could be done more efficiently in this manner. Also, some of the next steps could be electronically addressed and the process completed in a shorter time frame.)

2.0 All the cards are collected and grouped into a common area that comes from the group expectations at each level.

3.0 Topic-title cards are written, and the expectations are placed under the appropriate title.

4.0 Topic-title and related cards are written down in column form and shared with the faculty for their review.

5.0 Faculty groups at each level edit the topic columns and make changes as needed.

6.0 Faculty groups at each level come to consensus on the expectations under each title area.

This process results in the staff's producing curriculum expectations for any content area and level they wish to address within the school academic program. It is through this process of curriculum alignment that the faculty claim ownership of the curriculum, which is important for its implementation. This type of ownership leads to other area of investment—such as data gathering, data assessment, data analysis, and continual instructional improvement.

CURRICULUM SEQUENCE TO ENHANCE STUDENT LEARNING

The *curriculum sequence* is the order in which the content is addressed for the student's learning process. In many content areas, the order in which student expectations are studied is important to learning the subject. Reading and math are examples of content areas where sequence of student learning expectations are essential to student learning. In reading, basic letter sounds must be learned before words can be sounded out; students must learn letters before they can spell words. In math, knowing and understanding numbers must be in place to do basic operations such as adding and subtracting, which in turn must be mastered before learning multiplication and division.

Once the curriculum expectations are aligned by the faculty at various grade and course levels for the academic year, the faculty need to address the sequence of the content. The sequence of the content is the order in which it is taught through the academic year. The sequence of the material may enhance student learning especially if the content is progressive in nature. Building upon previously learned content helps students who are interested in learning reading and mathematics skills.

Aligning the curriculum should not be confused with sequence. Curriculum alignment is the process of relating different content areas so that students understand the relationships among these different areas. Curriculum sequence addresses the order in which content is covered and does not necessarily relate to integration with other content areas. That is not to say that these two concepts cannot work together to benefit the design of the curriculum.

CURRICULUM SCOPE AND DEPTH TO ENHANCE STUDENT LEARNING

Curriculum scope is the breadth to which the content is addressed in the instructional process at a particular level of study. The faculty are aware of the student mental development at each level and prepare instructional materials appropriate for the mental ability and capacity of the student group. Also, the depth of study is the extent of advanced knowledge the student is expected to study in the academic area. The faculty design the student academic expectations in such a manner as to develop cognitive skills with the scope and depth of knowledge in mind.

The scope and depth of an academic area at a particular level are designed to build on previous knowledge and prepare the student for future study in this area. At earlier levels of education, the student may be introduced to an idea that they later revisit in the educational process. In fact, many ideas are visited many times in the curriculum system, and the scope and depth are enhanced at each level. Some examples of scope and depth follow:

1. Reading is a skill that grows continually.
2. Mathematical scope of a concept such as probability is enhanced in more advanced courses such as statistics analysis and advanced probability.
3. Students are asked to sing basic melodies before moving on to difficult musical pieces.
4. Students are asked to analyze a short story before evaluating a novel.

SEQUENCE, SCOPE, AND DEPTH INTEGRATION IN THE CURRICULUM DESIGN

Many educators understand the sequence, scope, and depth integration of the curriculum as the *spy-role curriculum*. This concept introduces an idea at one point in the curriculum and brings it back into the curriculum later in the sequence at another level. This *spy-role* idea may revisit a concept or idea many times over various grade or course levels as the student progresses through the formal educational process.

VERTICAL INTEGRATION OF THE CURRICULUM

As students move through the academic program from grade to grade and course to course in a given subject area, the curriculum progresses in scope and depth. The faculty design the curriculum sequence and scope to enable students to build their knowledge and experience based on past levels of learning so that they can move confidently to future levels of knowledge. Vertical curriculum alignment assures the student of sequentially integrated systems of knowledge. Faculty coordinate the student academic expectations to blend from one level to another and create a seamless flow of content that enhances student learning of the subject area.

The curriculum-alignment process with respect to vertical integration is a powerful strategy that creates a wonderful opportunity for student mental development. Students need advanced mental challenges and vertical integration within the curriculum design. The following steps spell out one particular way the faculty can address this challenge.

1.0   Each faculty member writes down on 5" × 8" index cards each curricular expectation for the students' depth of knowledge at the content area and level at which it is desired.*

2.0   All the cards are collected and grouped into a common topic theme that comes from the group expectations.

3.0   Topic-title cards are written, and the expectations are placed under the appropriate topic title.

4.0   Topic title and related cards are written down in column form for the staff to review.

5.0   Faculty edit the topic columns and make changes as needed.

6.0   The faculty come to a consensus on the expectations under each title area.

7.0   Faculty review expectations with respect to the state standards at the content area and level being aligned.

8.0   Faculty integrate any state standard needing to be added to the expectations.

9.0   Faculty align different content areas that are related.

10.0   Faculty create a theme under which the aligned content can be taught.

11.0   Faculty create a time table for aligned themes (content) to be taught during the academic year.

12.0   Faculty coordinate time tables with academic levels above and below to align the content taught at various levels during the academic year.

13.0   Faculty develop units of study addressing the content that integrates the aligned expectations.

14.0   Faculty write out the final curriculum alignment in chart form for all teachers to see and follow.

  * This process could be electronically structured to save time.

CONTENT-INTEGRATED CURRICULUM DESIGN

Horizontal Integration of the Curriculum

Students explore many different subject areas at any given level in their schooling experience. Many subjects are taught with no concern for what other subjects are addressing at the same time. Faculty can horizontally integrate subject matter across different disciplines in order to enhance student understanding from multiple perspectives. If the faculty create a theme under which the unit of study is designed, many if not all of the different subjects might be related to this theme. Horizontal integration of academic objectives relates the content across different areas. A unit of study addressing the environment might relate science through weather patterns, math through creating charts and graphs of weather, reading through studying written documents and news reports of climate, writing through designing and presenting reports to the class on environmental patterns, social studies through climate impact on different areas of the country, art through different artists' interpretations of the topic, and so on.

Developing the scope of the curriculum is the challenge as the faculty looks at horizontal integration. Teaching the student to view an issue or concept from multiple perspectives is wonderful and challenging. For example, math and science courses may be horizontally organized to cover compatible concepts as each course is taught. Courses in physics and trigonometry may discuss the acceleration down an inclined plane and the different trigonometric functions to complement each other's understanding and demonstrate content integration of this material. Literature and social studies could read the same material and discuss writing style and historical and social significance within the two courses. Art and music can be studied during certain historical periods and related to social movements during those times. Many areas from different subjects can be horizontally integrated to enable multidimensional student learning and enhance higher cognitive levels of thinking. As students are required to think about issues from different perspectives, higher cognitive skills and mental processes can be addressed. (These thinking levels are addressed later in this chapter.)

1.0   Each faculty member at the same grade or course level writes down on 5" × 8" index cards each curriculum expectation for the students at the content area and level desired.*

2.0   All the cards are collected and grouped into a common topic theme that comes from the group expectations.

3.0   Topic-title cards are written, and the expectations are placed under the appropriate topic title.

4.0   Topic-title and related cards are written down in column form for the staff to review.

5.0   Faculty edit the topic columns and make changes as needed.

6.0   The faculty come to a consensus on the expectations under each title area.

7.0   Faculty review expectations with respect to the state standards at the content area and level being aligned.

8.0   Faculty integrate any state standard needing to be added to the expectations.

9.0   Faculty align different content areas horizontally that are related.

10.0   Faculty create a theme under which the aligned content can be taught.

11.0   Faculty create a time table for aligned themes to be taught during the academic year.

12.0   Faculty develop units of study addressing the themes that integrate the aligned expectations.

13.0   Real-life problem situations can be identified to address the curricular themes and concepts. Projects can be suggested to also address these same issues. (bie.org, 2014 and sfsu.edu, 2014)

14.0   As curricular expectations (themes and concepts) are identified, reverse designs can be determined to lead the students toward the final goals of the unit of study.

* This process could be electronically structured to save time.

CRITERIA FOR CURRICULAR EXPECTATIONS

Once the curriculum content is aligned with respect to sequence, scope, horizontal and vertical integration, and pacing, the faculty identify criteria for each student expectation. The faculty clarify each criterion by writing observable performance behaviors that meet the criterion. These observable performance criteria allow the faculty to evaluate whether or not each student has met learning expectations. Also, the instructional process can be evaluated to ascertain whether or not it meets expectations with respect to the student-learning process.

Curricular expectations are the established student-learning standards. Each expectation needs to be demonstrated by the student in some observable manner. Of course, the student is expected to learn to read, but the quality of the student's reading is what the teacher is to assess. Is the student's reading meeting the expectations? Clarifying the student expectation and the student's meeting the criteria by demonstrating the observable indicators are the answer to this question. Each student curricular expectation is assessed against the criteria relating to that expectation.

Student expectation

    Write a simple sentence

Criteria

    Correct spelling
    Correct punctuation
    Proper position of parts of speech

Student expectation

    Add simple fractions

Criteria

    Determine common denominator
    Determine numerator amounts
    Combine numerators
    Reduce to lowest terms

Student expectation

    Paint a natural setting in the woods with some trees using only the primary colors

Criteria

Primary colors are shown in the painting
Three secondary colors are shown in the painting
Trees are to show fall colors in the painting
Water stream and rocks are shown in the painting

OBSERVABLE INDICATORS FOR EACH CRITERION

The criteria indicators are the student behaviors assessed to determine the instructional system's effectiveness. These observable criteria indicators become the database used to study and assess the instructional and curriculum systems. As data are collected from the various criteria indictors, control charts can be created to analyze the system data and assess the effectiveness of the instructional and curriculum systems. In addition to the instructional-system analysis, the faculty can evaluate the student-performance data through control charts to determine student performance and overall curriculum-system success.

The faculty should continually analyze and evaluate the instructional and curricular systems to assess for efficacy. The faculty need to revise these systems when necessary and maintain those that are meeting expectations. The faculty's aim is to improve these systems continually through the database-gathering and -assessing process. The principal and faculty share this data analysis with all the professional staff and the community partners to enable continual improvement of the school academic program and benefit everyone in the schooling process.

Even though each criterion is stated to determine the student expectation for curricular content, it still may not be clear how the behavior of the student should be judged. Observable indicators may be necessary to determine the level of performance the student is to achieve with respect to the criteria. The *observable indicator* is the degree to which the student must meet each criterion identified under the curriculum expectation, as indicated below. In the first example, the student must spell every word correctly to meet the observable indicator and, therefore, that part of the criteria.

The *criteria* contain multiple parts as noted below:

Student expectation

Write a simple sentence

Criteria

Correct spelling (*indicator 100%*)
Correct punctuation (*indicator 100%*)
Proper position of parts of speech (*indicator 100%*)

Student expectation

Add simple fractions

Criteria

Determine common denominator (*indicator yes*)
Determine numerator amounts (*indicator yes*)
Combine numerators (*indicator yes*)
Reduce to lowest terms (*indicator no*)

Student expectation

Read an assigned paragraph at grade level

Criteria

Pronounce words correctly (*indicator 90%*)
Read punctuation properly (*indicator 90%*)
Read fluently (*indicator 50%*)
Comprehend material (*indicator 10%*)

The teacher must decide whether or not the level of performance meets the expectation. Once the student meets the expectation at the highest criteria, he or she has mastered that level of knowledge and goes on to the next level. The cognitive ability and capacity of the student along with the learning-style preference determines the achievement at any given time. The teacher must assess and analyze the student with respect to the content criteria and observable indicators to determine whether the student's performance is acceptable or requires additional instruction.

THEMATIC INTEGRATED-CURRICULUM DESIGN OF VARIOUS CONTENT AREAS

Integrated units of study can cross various content areas. A unit on Native American cultures might integrate social studies, language arts, art, and music. A unit covering industrial movement might integrate math, science, language arts, social studies, and other content areas. Each content area contributes knowledge to the unit goals and objectives. The faculty integrate the content so that students learn from multiple perspectives. The cognitive development of the student is the main goal, and each level of thinking—knowledge, comprehension, application, analysis, evaluation, and synthesis—is required in the units of study.

As the faculty integrate different content areas into a single unit of study, the student is given the opportunity to demonstrate higher-level thinking skills. Students are expected to apply knowledge, analyze different perspectives, synthesize information, and evaluate issues with respect to many criteria. Because the students are presented with multiple perspectives of information, they are required to view issues from many viewpoints. This is essential to each student's developing higher-level thinking.

After the faculty have aligned the curriculum horizontally and vertically, the faculty assesses areas in the content where relationships and common themes can be developed into units of study. This type of integration of content helps the student understand interrelationships in the material addressed and may develop higher levels of thinking.

1. Faculty who teach the same students and represent different content areas meet to plan integrated lessons that integrate various content areas.
2. Themes across the content are determined, and units of study are designed around these themes.

The goal of educating our children is to prompt them to think and make appropriate judgments that will enhance the quality of life for all.

Each unit of study not only advances knowledge of content but also advances thought. The goal of the curriculum is to create structures that enhance integrated learning and thinking. The concepts discussed in this section create a system to achieve this goal for our students. Each unit of study needs to include the following content:

1. Expectations for terminal student performance are established. This means that markers are established for measuring each student's demonstration of knowledge. Student knowledge can be demonstrated through various forms, such as written reports, research papers, artwork, projects, models, production pieces, drama work, and so on—whatever the faculty believe demonstrates and evaluates the quality of the student's learning, in other words. This student performance can be achieved through direct topic sequences, such as textbook instruction, project- or problem-based learning, any combination of these strategies, and whatever works for a given situation.

2. Cognitive objectives at each level of Bloom's taxonomy are required within the unit of study.

3. Learning-style activities are developed for each cognitive level.

4. Assessments for each cognitive level and for left- and right-brain processing are developed.

Once the thematic integrated-content unit is shared with the students, each student can move at his or her own pace and work independently and with other students to meet the expectations of the unit of study. Different learning stations and multiple resources are made available to the students. The teacher is also available to teach, review, mentor, and facilitate the learning process. As the units of study are completed, the students come together and share their outcomes and experiences from their studies. Each unit completion is a celebration of new learning, integration of knowledge, and experiences that each student gains from one another.

PROJECT BASED–LEARNING CURRICULUM DESIGN

Project-based learning is structured by the teacher, and projects are selected by the students. Project-based learning states the student outcome expectations and structures many of the instructional strategies the student must complete. The teacher structures many mini teaching sessions to address project content and student issues while doing these projects. The student can work independently or in work groups to complete the project.

The teacher is available to instruct, coach, mentor, and advise when needed. Time lines are set and assessment criteria predetermined by the teacher. The aim of this curriculum design is to give the student more responsibility for his or her own learning and management of time as well as facilitate student creativity in how the project is completed and how criteria-assessment expectations set for the project are met.

PROBLEM BASED–LEARNING CURRICULUM DESIGN

Problem-based learning exemplifies the trend toward a more collaborative relationship between teacher and learner. In this model, the teacher and student are copartners in the curricular process. The student takes responsibility for his or her own learning, there are few lectures and little structured sequence of assigned materials, collaboration is fostered among students, and solving a problem within the context of the real world is stressed. The characteristics of the curriculum design are:

1. developing analytical problem-solving skills
2. determining the knowledge needed to understand the problem being investigated
3. researching the best resources for acquiring knowledge about the problem
4. doing one's own research to understand and study the problem
5. applying one's researched information and knowledge to solve the problem
6. and creating and presenting solutions to the problem (sfsu.edu, 2014)

The problem-based learning process addresses three general phases:

1. What do we already know about the problem?
2. What do we need to know to solve the problem?
3. What do we need to do to solve the problem? (bie.org, 2014)

The aim of the problem-based curriculum is to have students develop applied competence, critical-thinking skills, problem-solving competence, and collaborative and leadership competence. This model is consistent with the direction in which teaching and learning is trending and allows more student responsibility for learning and support from teachers in a more collaborative role. With the advent of resource availability through current technologies, students can gain information and knowledge beyond what the traditional classroom has to offer. Teaching and learning is becoming a true partnership between teachers and learners.

As problem-based curricula are completed, alignment to common-core state standards is assessed and completed. As additional standards are to be addressed, additional problems are identified and investigated to cover particular standards. The curriculum may be a combination of problem-based studies as well as all the other options shared in this chapter.

CURRICULUM SYSTEM SURVEY

3.0   Curriculum System

    3.1   *Professional staff understand the process of curriculum alignment.* The process of the curriculum alignment reflects vertical and horizontal networks that address student-learning needs and expectations. (Vertical networks coordinate content area expectations in sequential order from prekindergarten through twelfth grade, math sequence from prekindergarten through twelfth grade.) Horizontal networks integrate content area expectations through all content areas by grade level (math, science, social studies, language arts, art, music, etc.). The alignment process determines the sequence and scope of the curriculum and is the framework for the instructional system.

        1   2   3   4   5   6   7   8   9

3.2   *Professional staff align curricular expectations hori-zontally.* Curricular expectations are integrated across a grade level with respect to content areas. This content integration allows students to synthesize their knowledge. Many students are not able to integrate information unless it is presented in a manner that relates these different perspectives together. Knowledge from different content areas at the same level can be aligned to enhance student integration of the material.

    1   2   3   4   5   6   7   8   9

3.3   *Professional staff align curricular expectations vertically.* Curricular expectations are sequenced throughout the academic program to build and support each other. The faculty analyze each level of expectations to assure that they build upon previous levels. Each academic grade and course blends with the one before and after, creating a flow of expectations that enhances student learning.

    1   2   3   4   5   6   7   8   9

3.4   *Professional staff integrate state academic standards into curricular expectations to determine grade- and course-level student expectations.* District grade- and course-level curricular expectations are aligned and state academic standards integrated to determine student academic expectations at each level in the district academic program. Student academic expectations may exceed state standards, which are viewed as basic at each level. District and school curricula are the blueprint for student learning. The state standards are the minimum guidelines that must be addressed within the school curriculum.

    1   2   3   4   5   6   7   8   9

3.5   *Professional staff write grade- and course-level expectations relating and integrating various content areas of study.* The staff develop and write units of study that incorporate student academic expectations from different content areas of study. An example of relating content areas with respect to the study of the environment is graphing population growth in mathematics, reading about culture in language arts and the social sciences, and examining geological formations in science. The unit of study would relate this information in a manner enabling students to understand the interrelationships of this material.

1   2   3   4   5   6   7   8   9

3.6   *Professional staff integrate levels of critical thinking within content areas of study.* As the unit of study is developed, each of the cognitive levels of critical thinking is designed into the unit. Activities based on the unit content are designed to require each student to know, comprehend, apply, analyze, synthesize, and evaluate information within the area of study.

1   2   3   4   5   6   7   8   9

3.7   *Professional staff organize curriculum sequence to enhance student learning.* Curricular expectations are sequenced horizontally and vertically within and across content areas to enable students to understand interrelationships and draw larger meaning from their study. The sequence of learning knowledge may enhance student ability to understand and grow academically. Based on research and experience, the faculty sequence the curriculum in a manner most beneficial to each student's learning style and capacity.

1   2   3   4   5   6   7   8   9

3.8   *Professional staff organize curriculum scope to enhance student learning.* The depth of each curricular expectation is designed into the units of study to enable each student to gain new knowledge based on previously learned information. As students move from learning unit to learning unit, grade level to grade level, school to school, the curriculum flows in a manner that builds student knowledge and understanding.

1   2   3   4   5   6   7   8   9

3.9   *Professional staff write criteria for each curricular expectation.* Criteria for each curricular expectation are written to communicate to the faculty and students the level of knowledge needed to demonstrate acceptable evidence of student learning. Criteria are used to assess the instructional process and student performance on critical expectations. Unless criteria are clear, the staff are not able to understand whether or not students are learning and the instructional process is achieving its aim.

1   2   3   4   5   6   7   8   9

3.10   *Professional staff write observable indicators for criteria to determine student performance with respect to each student-learning expectation.* Each criterion needs specific observable indicators to identify student-learned knowledge. These indicators are the basis for data gathering and analysis, which allow for continual instructional and academic improvement. The improvement process is totally dependent on this issue being addressed and implemented. If it is not implemented, the entire continual-improvement philosophy is undermined and the continual improvement process will fail.

1   2   3   4   5   6   7   8   9

CHAPTER 5

Instruction System

System: Instruction
System aim: Present the curriculum
Methodology: Whatever works

The instruction system is the *method used* by the professional staff to present the curriculum system to the students. It is through these *methods of instruction* that the professional staff educate their students. Many people in our country believe that our educational system can be improved through high-stakes testing programs. These strategies are not working and are actually delaying the process of instructional improvement. Student academic expectations are achieved through continual improvement of the instructional process.

As different instructional strategies are implemented, data need to be gathered from these strategies and from student performance. Then these data need to be assessed against specific criterion indicators. With the assistance of the faculty and students, instructional-process improvements can be made and the new strategies implemented in the next cycle.

Again, student data are gathered and assessed to determine strategy improvement and system performance. Only through analysis of the instructional processes is improvement of student learning determined. Testing student performance tells you where the student is but does not help you determine how to improve the teaching and learning process. Analyzing the instructional process brings new knowledge to the teaching-learning process. If the system of instruction is viewed as a continual-improvement process, we have a better chance of achieving what the professional staff expect from the student-learning process.

The instructional system contains many strategies such as direct instruction, small-group discussion, one-on-one tutoring, indirect instruction, large-group instruction, interest-group study, peer-group instruction, project-based learning, and problem-based learning, among many others. The bottom line is that the faculty need to understand that the instructional system is the only system over which they have significant control and that it is the one that needs to be improved in order to enhance student achievement. The method of instruction is the key to student performance. If you change the instructional method, you change student performance.

Teachers need to research the methods used to instruct their students and continually improve these methods. This is the way student performance can be improved in the future. Some of the steps teachers need to implement to research instructional methods follow:

1. Clarify student expectations in the area being taught.
2. State specific criteria for the student expectations.
3. Identify observable indicators on which data will be collected.
4. Determine the method of instruction to be researched.
5. Determine the method of collecting data.
6. Determine the method of data analysis.
7. Implement the method of instruction under the conditions agreed upon.
8. Record data at times agreed upon during the implementation of the method.
9. Record student-performance data after the method time limit is used.
10. Analyze *methodology data.*
11. Analyze *student-performance data.*
12. Conclude from data findings the results of the study.
13. Recommend revisions of the *instructional methods* for the future.

Planning instructional experiences is challenging and exciting. Many elements are involved in planning a challenging study. Once the curriculum and state standards are addressed, the teacher envisions a unit of study that captures these expectations in an integrated manner and presents it in such a way as to challenge and invest the students. Getting students excited about learning is an art form. Sharing real-life experiences that demonstrate the knowledge to be learned is one way to help students understand why this knowledge is valuable. If students see no reason to learn something, why would they give their time to it?

Planning a good introduction to a lesson is essential to creating a positive atmosphere and attitude for student learning. When problems and projects are presented with an excellent introductory strategy, stating clear learning expectations, requiring thinking at different levels, designing alternative-learning activities, offering alternative-assessment strategies, expecting students to solve problems and complete projects, and including other activities that demonstrate expected learned knowledge, students can get excited about learning.

Planning a real-life conceptual and application study demands faculty cooperation and collaboration. The time that is required to complete this task can be overwhelming if left to an individual teacher. Teamwork is essential if this task is to be achieved and implemented consistently for students to benefit. Many of the specific elements of a quality unit of study are addressed in the following material.

PREPARING STUDENTS FOR CHALLENGING LEARNING EXPERIENCES

1. *Prepare the students for the concepts and areas of study.* The teacher presents activities that gain the student's attention on the concepts to be learned. These activities provide a readiness for the material about to be studied. Previously learned ideas and practices are integrated into these activities to motivate the student for new learning and new activities. This allows the teacher to informally assess the student's knowledge of the area to be studied.

2. *Establish learning expectations and the purposes of this study.* Student-learning expectations and purposes for learning inform the student as to what they are able to do after completing the material studied and why this knowledge is important, useful, and relevant for the future. This might be the opportunity to pretest the students on the future lesson expectations.

3. *Determine instructional methods.* Present the curricular concepts and content and instructional activities needed to achieve student learning.
4. *Model the student expectation if needed.* Present finished products and demonstrate processes so students see examples of expectations they are to achieve. Either the teacher or the student can do the modeling.
5. *Check for understanding during the process.* The teacher requires that the student demonstrate essential information and critical skills and the knowledge expected in the student-learning expectation.
6. *Guide practice for the student to expand experiences.* Allow practice time for the student to perform the tasks taught to determine learning or if redirect teaching is necessary. This practice time to demonstrate learning must be in the presence of the teacher so immediate correction is given if needed.
7. *Allow for additional applications to solve problems.* The student is given additional practice of learned material to develop fluency, competence, and confidence in what has been learned.

These elements are the instructional methods the teacher uses to communicate with the student to create an atmosphere for learning. Each element gives different learners an opportunity to get involved in a manner comfortable to them. Options for learning are the keys to involving the students and getting them excited about learning (Joyce and Showers 1983).

UNIT-STUDY DESIGN ELEMENTS AND INTEGRATION OF CONTENT AREAS: UNIT OF STUDY DESIGN SYSTEM LEVELS

1. Concept theme agreed upon by staff members teaching the unit of study
2. Integration of various content areas included in the unit
3. Student performance expectations (unit terminal student outcomes)
4. Student performance expectations at each cognitive level
5. Student learning-style activities (all four styles)

6. Student-assessment strategies for each cognitive level, terminal outcomes, and right- and left-hemisphere thinking process and unit-outcome objectives

Content integration among different subject-matter areas allows the student to relate knowledge from many perspectives. One goal teachers intend to achieve is student integrated thinking. Lessons have to be designed to create multiple lenses through which students view knowledge and integrate and analyze ideas. Content from different areas of study should be aligned conceptually to enable students' thinking and relational perceptions about these ideas. Many math and science concepts can be integrated in a lesson. For example, the relationship of a right triangle in math and the incline plane in physics can be integrated.

There are so many opportunities for concepts and topics to be related to enhance student thinking that it is not difficult to do so. Thematic units of study are excellent examples of integrating concepts across many content areas. This design strategy enables the student to relate knowledge from multiple content areas and study relationships between each other and understand issues from a global perspective. Helping students think through an integrated perspective is one way to develop higher-level thinking skills. Is this not one of the major goals of our educational process and an expectation we have of our curricular and instructional systems?

Students need to integrate information from various areas of content so they understand the interrelationships and interdependencies of things. Teachers can facilitate this integration of content in the following ways:

1. Align the curriculum content areas of related topics at the same time.
2. Sequence content across different content areas to allow integration.
3. Design thematic units of study.
4. Integrate specific courses such as math and science, social studies and literature.
5. Team teach across two different content areas.
6. Identify themes around which teachers can align content.
7. Collaborate with other teachers on lesson design.

8. Use a common event as a focal point for different subjects to address.
9. Brainstorm ideas with the faculty for areas of integration.
10. Design project-based curriculum strategies to create knowledge integration.
11. Design problem-based curriculum strategies to create knowledge integration.

ORGANIZE THE ENVIRONMENT FOR LEARNING

Organizational structures within the classroom can facilitate learning. Different structures enhance modes of instruction. Theater seating is appropriate for large-group lectures when teacher information sharing is the objective. This forum is excellent for showing films, videos, PowerPoint presentations, and giving lectures.

Table arrangements are excellent for small-group discussions, learning-station materials, focus-group activities, follow-up after lecture sessions, and other small group–process activities.

Study stations are excellent for individual-student private time. A number of private-study stations should be available in the classroom for students to use when needed.

The learning environment needs to be flexible to enable achievement of the learning expectations. Various classroom arrangements are necessary to meet different student-learning styles. The teacher needs to create a learning atmosphere in which each student finds it comfortable to learn. Along with the different modes of instruction, student-learning styles need to be accommodated in the learning environment.

MODES OF LEARNING: VIRTUAL AND FACE-TO-FACE

1. Large-group instruction
2. Small-group discussion
3. Independent study
4. Tutorial instruction
5. Peer instruction
6. Collaborative-task groups

INSTRUCTIONAL MATERIALS APPROPRIATE
FOR VARIOUS STUDENT NEEDS

A wide range of learning materials is needed in any learning environment. At least three reading levels exist in most grade-level classrooms, and determining a student's reading level is critical to enhancing learning. In order for the teacher to address different learning levels and styles, many types of materials need to be available in the learning environment. These instructional materials include internet links to websites, videos, workbooks, other texts, posters, artworks, music pieces, multilevel texts, audiotapes, drawing materials, interactive activities, self-learning activities, group action games, self-evaluation feedback activities, and so on.

One of the most critical aspects of teaching is determining the level of material most appropriate for effective learning of each student. Once a student starts to experience success in learning new information, lights go on and self-concepts are reinforced. When a student experiences the joy of learning, the joy of teaching follows, and both parties benefit.

The current diversity of the student population is greater than ever before and is going to continue to grow. We are saving more children today through medical technology than we ever have in past years. These children are coming to our schools and creating more demanding and wider ranges of instructional strategies. The student needs are greater, and the instructional options must be wide open for what works for any given child.

With technology advancing as it is today, many methods of instruction are being tested and implemented to assist student learning. It is incumbent upon the teacher to provide multiple ways of learning any new information in the learning environment today. Not only do different levels of material need to be available for the student, different modes and sources must be available within the learning environment for immediate access. Therefore, schools and communities must unite to keep up with future demands for learning opportunities within, as well as outside of, the school building.

STUDENT-LEARNING EXPECTATIONS

Student-learning expectations are shared at the beginning of each new learning area of study to clarify what is expected of the student. These expectations clarify the purpose of the study and help the student understand the concepts and content to be learned. Many times students do not know what is expected of them and are not clear as to how learning activities fit into the study. An excitement for learning can be created by the teacher's explanation of what is going to be studied and some of the ways learning is going to take place. Also, demonstrating the useful application of what is going to be learned can excite students as to why it is important to study this new knowledge.

The student must know what is expected in the area of study. A good way to remember what needs to be clear to the student is to state student expectations for learning using the *A-B-C-D method*, using the following format:

1. *Audience*: The student is the audience
2. *Behavior*: The specific behavior to be demonstrated by the student
3. *Conditions*: The circumstances under which the expectations are demonstrated
4. *Degree*: The level of proficiency the student is to achieve

Some examples of student-learning expectations following this format follow.

The student will write a paragraph demonstrating proper use of grammar, spelling, and main-idea and supporting-sentence design in class within fifteen minutes with no errors in grammar, spelling, sentence structure, and paragraph design.

Audience: The student
Behavior: will write a paragraph demonstrating proper use of grammar, spelling, and main-idea and supporting-sentence design
Conditions: in class within fifteen minutes
Degree: with no errors in grammar, spelling, sentence structure, and paragraph design (in other words, 100 percent correct)

The student will demonstrate an understanding of the Pythagorean Theorem to locate and draw a right angle with the vertex at a designated point on the floor of the classroom, given a piece of chalk and a stick three feet in length within fifteen minutes from the time the teacher gives the student the materials.

Audience: The student

Behavior: will demonstrate an understanding of the Pythagorean Theorem to locate and draw a right angle with the vertex at a designated point on the floor of the classroom

Conditions: given a piece of chalk and a stick three feet in length and within fifteen minutes from the time the teacher gives the student the materials

Degree: No degree is stated in the expectation, and therefore the task must be done 100 percent, or the student does not achieve the expectation

The student will synthesize four editorial articles on the same topic into a one-page article of two hundred words using the computer in a fifty-minute class period. The paper will be assessed for content, grammar, spelling, sentence structure, and design. A total of three errors or less is acceptable.

Audience: The student

Behavior: will synthesize four editorial articles on the same topic

Conditions: into a one-page article of two hundred words using the computer in a fifty-minute class period

Degree: Total of three errors or less on content, grammar, spelling, sentence structure, and design

STUDENT ACTIVITIES DESIGNED FOR EACH COGNITIVE LEVEL

One of the most important goals of our educational system is to promote each student's development in the ability to analyze and problem solve.[1] Thinking is developed through instructional activities that mentally challenge the mind and cause a student to question existing ideas and concepts. Learning is a function of knowledge and experience. The more a student is challenged with new experiences and problems to be analyzed and solved, the more the thinking process is developed to face additional challenges.

STRATEGIES TO FACILITATE STUDENT ACTIVITIES
FOR EACH LEARNING STYLE

Learning environments need to be designed to facilitate different types of learning. Some students need structure, some need less structure, some need movement, and some need quiet time. Each student has a style of learning that is most beneficial to him or her for processing new information. The learning environment needs to create options for learning that address the four major learning styles: concrete sequential, abstract random, abstract sequential, and concrete random.

Concrete sequential: Present experiences in a sequential linear, structured, ordered, hands-on, immediately reinforced, and teacher-centered manner.

Abstract random: Present active experiences, small-group, multiple-source, unstructured, and student-centered discussion.

Abstract sequential: Present ideas in a sequence using written lists, order, logic, conceptual approaches, and teacher-centered approaches.

Concrete random: Present ideas and discuss, using movement, action, hands-on methods, observation, experimentation, and student-centered methods.

The learning environment needs to address each student style so new information is presented in a manner receptive to the student. Students should not only learn knowledge in their primary style, but they should also be required to experience different styles of learning. If a student learns most effectively as a concrete sequential, after the initial presentation in that style the student should be required to be in a small-group discussion (abstract random) to reinforce the understanding of new material. If a student learns most effectively through group discussion (abstract random), the follow-up style might be abstract sequential, which would require reading material on the topic discussed earlier.

The goal of designing a quality unit of study is to enable and enhance each student's opportunity for learning through various styles of learning and expand the integrated knowledge base.

INSTRUCTIONAL ACTIVITIES BASED ON STUDENT LEARNING STYLES

Concrete sequential

Student activities: Workbooks, lab manuals, drawings, models, demonstrations, hands-on materials, field trips, programmed materials, assisted materials, step-by-step instruction, drill activities, practice sessions on learned materials, correct answers from assessment activities

Student attributes: Accepts teacher authority and expects the teacher to maintain control in the learning environment; has a very low tolerance for distraction in the learning environment, especially when new material is being presented for the first time

Abstract random

Student activities: Movies, videos, discussions in small groups, lecture followed by small-group discussion, short in-class readings with discussion, learning from fellow students through discussion, hearing ideas from discussion, hearing themselves express ideas to assess their understanding of the material

Student attributes: Aware of colors, sounds, and modes in the classroom environment, observes body language, listens critically to tone of expression in connection with the message being delivered; very reflective and willing to change position after further discussion on an issue; delivery of message is extremely important for integration and learning; dislikes teacher control and likes a busy environment; able to concentrate with many activities going on in the learning environment at the same time

Abstract sequential

Student activities: Textbook and other reading materials, audiotapes, extensive reading assignments, lecture, debate, written assignments, logical-reasoning activities

Student attributes: Able and willing to read large amounts of material and understand the ideas and concepts, able to express ideas and convey them orally and in writing, has a wealth of mental pictures, able to develop hypothetical and theoretical positions and to analyze and evaluate well; very logical and content-oriented and demands documentation in order to be influenced; respects teacher authority and has a very low tolerance for distraction in the learning environment

Concrete random

Student activities: Games and simulations, independent study, optional reading assignments, mini-lectures, problem-solving activities, project applications, action activities

Student attributes: Able to formulate hypothetical positions, develop alternative solutions and test them to solve problems, develop practical application of ideas to solve problems; willing to experiment through application, not concerned about following format, willing to take risks to problem solve a situation; uncomfortable with firm structure and authority in classroom and dislikes limitations on learning alternatives; enjoys rich active learning environment when learning. (Gregoric 1979)

PACE SEQUENCE AND DETERMINE SCOPE AND DEPTH OF LESSONS TO ENHANCE STUDENT LEARNING

The faculty at each level of instruction must agree on the sequence of learning objectives and the scope of instruction. Sequence of student expectations in the units of study and lessons taught is critical to student mental development. The instructional strategies used by the teacher integrate the sequence of learning objectives, scope of the learning objectives, appropriate learning materials, and structures within the learning environment to enhance student learning.

Based on the concept of building a consistent curriculum model at each level of instruction, the scope and depth of knowledge addressed at a particular level of instruction is agreed upon by the faculty. The scope and depth of an objective at a particular level are determined by the horizontal and vertical integration of the curriculum. It is for this very reason that the entire faculty must be involved in the alignment of the curriculum and in the design of the grade- and course-level units of study. Without this faculty perspective and knowledge, the overall instructional system will not result in continuity from one level to the next for the student.

Pacing of instruction is the time sequence given to presenting, explaining, practicing, and evaluating student learning of new information. Pacing the sequence of instructional methods is critical for the student to internalize the information being taught. If the new material is taught too quickly, the student will not understand the information and learning will not occur. This may cause the teacher to reteach the material, which proper pacing would have prevented.

If the pacing is too slow, the student will get bored, which creates many other problems in the classroom. Even though pacing the instructional lesson is designed into the lesson, the teacher must continually judge student learning as students are learning the new information. Teacher sensitivity to learning and continual assessment of the students on the new information are required if pacing is going to be correct for the lesson.

As the students are asked to demonstrate the new knowledge, the teacher assesses their understanding through work samples, seatwork, answering questions, explaining ideas in their own words, in-class assignments, and homework assignments. Pacing for maximum learning efficiency and effectiveness is a judgment made by the teacher continually. Pacing of instruction is an art as much as it is a science.

Another way a teacher can assess pacing of instruction is to ask the students how it is going. The students can tell the teacher whether or not they feel things are moving too fast and explain what needs to be given more time. Even though the teacher is using other methods to check the pace of the lesson, discussing the pacing with the students gives them a sense of involvement in the teaching and learning process.

Scope of instruction is the depth of the new information the teacher decides to address in the instructional process. The depth of instruction needs to align itself with the total curriculum, and each teacher needs to respect the agreements made in the alignment process. Each grade level and course builds on the previous one, and the sequence and depth of any content area is part of a larger system of integrated knowledge. This laddering effect is critical to the success of the overall curriculum system and the teaching process to enhance student learning.

The scope and depth of instruction also need to respect the cognitive ability and capacity of the students. As a student grows older, the brain develops and is capable of more advanced levels of thinking. However, at earlier ages the student may not be able to handle certain tasks because he or she is not yet ready for the task. If the scope of the material is too difficult, the student may experience a high level of frustration and be turned off from learning. The fear is that the student may also perceive that he or she is not capable of learning and that his or her self-concepts may be destroyed.

GUIDED PRACTICE

Guided practice is critical for student learning. Once new learning material has been presented, the teacher provides the student with an opportunity to demonstrate the new knowledge. It is through this practice that the teacher determines whether or not the student has learned the new knowledge. Guided practice needs to follow instruction and be given in the presence of the teacher so correction can take place immediately. Guided practice allows the student to clarify misunderstandings of the new material and reinforces learned knowledge.

Guided practice can take place in many forms in the learning environment. Students may be asked to work on their own, in small groups, or in an integration of the two. The teacher is able to assess the students' learning through guided practice and determine whether or not additional teaching is needed to help the students understand the new information. If the teacher does not check the student's understanding of this new knowledge, the student may leave the classroom applying this knowledge in an inappropriate manner.

This could lead the student to a misunderstanding of this new knowledge and a need for additional teaching to unlearn bad habits or wrong application of knowledge. Both the student and teacher suffer in this situation because of wasted time and effort, not to mention the reteaching and relearning that must occur. Reteaching is not a negative behavior and is welcomed as review sessions for students as needed often throughout the year. However, if reteaching is caused by the teacher's not pacing or checking for understanding or proper application, it is wasted instructional time.

If the teacher covers new material and does not have the opportunity to provide guided practice for the students, the teacher should not assign any homework or application of the new material until guided practice can be provided. This gets back to pace and scope of the instructional methods used to teach the students. Guided practice must precede independent practice, and the teacher is in control of this sequence of events. The student can benefit from a well-disciplined teacher who implements the steps of a well-planned lesson.

INSTRUCTIONAL STRATEGIES HAVING THE HIGHEST IMPACT ON LEARNING

Identifying similarities and differences

Comparing: Identifying similarities and differences between and among things or ideas

Classifying: Grouping things that are alike into categories on the basis of their characteristics

Creating metaphors: Identifying a general or basic pattern in a specific topic and then finding another topic that appears to be quite different but that has the same general pattern

Creating analogies: Identifying relationships between pairs of concepts—in other words, identifying relationships between relationships

Summarizing

To summarize effectively, one must delete some information, substitute some information, and keep some information.

Delete material that is unnecessary to understand.

Delete redundant material.

Substitute superordinate terms for lists.

Select a topic sentence, or invent one if it is missing.

Note taking

Verbatim note taking is the least-effective way to take notes.

Notes should be considered a work in progress.

Notes should be used as study guides for tests.

The more notes that are taken, the better.

Format notes using outlines, webbing, and a combination of the two.

Reinforcing effort

Not all students realize the importance of believing in effort.

Students can learn to change their beliefs to an emphasis on effort.

Providing recognition

Rewards do not necessarily have a negative effect on intrinsic motivation.

Reward is most effective when it is contingent on the attainment of some standard performance.

Abstract symbolic recognition is more effective than tangible rewards (Marzano, Pickering, and Pollock 2005.)

PROBLEM- AND PROJECT-BASED LEARNING PROCESSES

Problem- and project-based learning instructional strategies rely on student direction, self-pacing, and self-discovery. The process begins with the teacher presenting the student with a problem or project to be addressed. The teacher acts as a facilitator and mentor in the process of student learning. The student is in total control as he or she studies whatever is needed to solve the problem or complete the project.

1. The student explores the issues related to the problem or project. It is up to the student to define the problem, analyze the problem, and gather information related to the problem.
2. What does the student know to solve the problem? The student determines what he or she knows and what other team members know related to the problem.
3. The student redefines the problem and creates a problem statement in his or her own words. This problem statement is a draft position and is subject to continual revision as the study of the problem advances.

4. The student writes a draft of the possible solutions to the problem, ranking the solutions as the student thinks of them from the best to the least-possible solution.

5. The student creates action plans to solve the problem. How do each of the action plans relate to the solutions to the problem? Does the team come to agreement as to the action plan to solve the problem?

6. What else does the team need to know, and whom does the team need to consult in order to fill in any needed information? What other resources does the team need to study? What deadlines need to be addressed? If the team is convinced of the solution and has the needed support for this solution based on the research and other data, move to the next step. If the team is not convinced of the solution and the support data, go back and repeat steps 4, 5, and 6, starting with analyzing additional possible solutions.

7. The student writes up the solution with research-based documentation and submits it to the team and revises it based on the feedback. The student presents the research study to the other students and reports on the process and findings, stating any conclusions. Based on the presentation, the student revises the report and addresses any issues that need to be taken into account. After the final report is revised, it is presented to the teacher.

8. The student reflects on the research study and assesses what went well and what could be improved upon in the future. Feedback and analysis is asked of the team also (Study Guides and Strategies, 1996).

INSTRUCTIONAL-SYSTEM SURVEY

4.0   Instruction system

   4.1   *Professional staff understand instruction is the method to achieving academic improvement.* Instruction is the method teachers use to stimulate student interest and enhance learning. Through various instructional strategies, teachers create an environment in which student learning comes alive. Instruction is the means by which the teacher leads the student to achieve the academic expectations stated in the school curriculum. Instruction is the means to the academic aim, which is student learning. Continual improvement of instruction is the method by which continual improvement of student learning is achieved.

1   2   3   4   5   6   7   8   9

4.2   *Teachers plan the instructional lessons.* The faculty plan instructional lessons to facilitate student learning through classroom activities. Lessons consist of objectives, teaching strategies, guided student practice, reteaching strategies as needed, follow-up activities, and student products meeting previously established criteria to assure learning.

1   2   3   4   5   6   7   8   9

4.3   *Teachers integrate content areas in the learning lesson when possible.* Content-area integration enables students to synthesize information and view issues from multiple perspectives. Often this content integration can be accomplished through a thematic unit. The aim is to relate different areas of knowledge in such a manner as to allow the student to integrate ideas and understand these relationships.

1   2   3   4   5   6   7   8   9

4.4   *Teachers organize the environment for learning.* Classroom organization can facilitate different types of learning. Different structures enhance different modes of instruction (theater seating for large-group lecture, table groupings for small-group discussion, and individual learning stations for independent study). If the learning environment is structured for different learning styles, students can use multiple opportunities to learn the same information. Also, a student may use his or her primary learning style to learn difficult material and reinforce learning through a secondary style. Some students may enjoy learning new knowledge through various learning styles and welcome the options made available within the environment.

1   2   3   4   5   6   7   8   9

4.5   *Teachers provide instructional materials appropriate for various student needs.* Teachers provide appropriate materials for student reading levels, motor abilities, hearing capacities, physical skills, and many other needs. As diversity increases in the student body, alternative materials to meet these diverse student needs are essential. Instructional materials of different modes and levels are required in every instructional setting. One cannot know which type of instructional material is most helpful for any student at any given time.

1   2   3   4   5   6   7   8   9

4.6   *Teachers clarify student-learning expectations for the instructional lesson.* Teachers clarify student-learning expectations at the beginning of each lesson. These expectations are determined by the curriculum system and are stated in the units of study developed by the faculty. Students should be aware of the academic expectations in advance to give direction and purpose to the learning experience. In addition to the students, parents and other interested parties may wish to know student academic expectations, and this information can be made available when requested.

1   2   3   4   5   6   7   8   9

4.7   *Teachers implement strategies to facilitate student activities for each cognitive level.* The teacher implements instructional strategies to facilitate student involvement at each cognitive level: knowledge, comprehension, application, analysis, synthesis, and evaluation. The strategies selected by the teacher create the opportunity for students to develop thinking skills at each cognitive level.

1   2   3   4   5   6   7   8   9

4.8   *Teachers implement strategies to facilitate student activities for each learning style.* Four major learning styles are reported continually in the educational research: concrete-sequential thinking (hands on and step by step), abstract-random thinking (auditory and nonsequential), abstract-sequential thinking (written and step by step), and concrete-random thinking (hands on and nonsequential). Each student learning expectation is taught in multiple ways to enable students to learn through these different learning styles. The learning environment is designed with different learning stations that allow for alternative learning-style instruction for students.

1   2   3   4   5   6   7   8   9

4.9   *Teachers pace the sequence and determine the scope of the lesson to enhance student learning.* The order and depth given to instruction are critical to the student's ability to learn. Each student has his or her own time schedule for learning. Sequence and depth of instructional materials are designed to cover the student expectations. Different student abilities and capacities are met through the appropriate planning and implementing of sequencing and pacing instruction. Also, the depth to which each student studies the learning expectations is determined by his or her ability and capacity. The teachers address all of these factors in planning instructional lessons.

1   2   3   4   5   6   7   8   9

4.10   *Teachers provide guided practice to determine student learning or the need for reteaching.* After the teacher completes instruction of new material, time is given for students to practice what they have learned. This practice time is guided by the teacher to determine whether or not the student meets or perhaps exceeds academic expectations or if the student needs additional instruction to encourage learning. Based on the teacher's findings, different learning-style materials and pacing may be implemented to enhance student learning. Assessing the student's knowledge through guided practice is critical for deciding the next move to benefit student growth.

1   2   3   4   5   6   7   8   9

NOTE

1. See the common core of critical-thinking levels in chapter 4.

CHAPTER 6

Assessment System

System: Assessment of instruction strategies and student performance
System Aim: Continually improve instructional strategies and student
achievement
Methodology: Statistically analyze instructional strategies and student
achievement

SYSTEMS DATA GATHERED THROUGH ACTION-RESEARCH STUDIES AND OTHER SOURCES

The assessment system is the evaluation of the instruction and student-achievement and performance systems. Through the assessment system, the professional staff are able to gather and analyze data to determine the effectiveness of the instructional process and student academic performance. This analysis is essential to improving the methods of the instruction and improvement of student academic performance.

ASSESSMENT OF INSTRUCTIONAL AND PERFORMANCE SYSTEMS

1. After student-curriculum expectations are clarified, specific student observable indicators are identified under each of the expectations.
2. Assessment strategies are then created to determine student achievement on each of the observable indicators.
3. After data are gathered on the observable indicators, they are analyzed using statistical control charts, and the professional staff determine trends in the data.

4. After normal and special causes of variation are identified, the staff implement changes in the instructional system to improve student academic performance.

5. Assessments of instructional methods, as well as student performance, are analyzed with the aim of continually improving both systems.

6. After assessment information is shared with the school staff, the instructional teams analyze the data and suggest improvements for the academic programs.

7. It is through these assessments that the academic programs are evaluated and the professional staff and community members can be assured that the quality of education given to the students is meeting expectations.

8. After the academic program–improvement recommendations are received, reviewed, analyzed, and evaluated by the school academic-planning team, the team can consider making recommendations to the school-improvement planning process team for future school-improvement planning.

SCHOOL AND COMMUNITY PARTNERSHIPS

Assessment of academic-program data in its various forms is the method of accountability that communities are looking for to assure academic quality. As partnerships are created between professional staff and community members to share and understand academic-program expectations and results, opportunities for collaboration and cooperation to build better learning options for everyone are established. Everyone in the community is valued as each person works to build a better learning environment for each person to benefit.

CRITICAL STEPS: CLARIFY STANDARDS, CRITERIA, DATA-GATHERING, AND ANALYSIS PROCESS

As stated previously in chapter 4, student expectations must be clarified. Once the student expectations are clear, assessment structures must be designed to determine the achievement levels of the students on each of the expectations. This assessment process involves stating criteria and observable indicators under each of the curricular expectations, which are assessed. However, this is not the only assessment necessary to determine how to affect student results. The instructional process itself has to be assessed to determine whether or not it can be changed to improve student learning and, therefore, student academic achievement.

It is for this very reason that teachers must collaborate on the instructional methods used to teach a particular set of student expectations. Unless the teachers determine and analyze specific instructional strategies, the aim of improving instruction is not possible. If the methods are not assessed, the results mean nothing. Students can be achieving excellent results without it having anything to do with instruction at all. How would we know?

Only as the faculty gather, analyze, and discuss data with respect to instructional strategies are the opportunities for improvement possible. This is a major challenge for the faculty because it addresses the heart of the instructional process. It asks the faculty to remove its ego from the process and look at the assessment of instruction in an objective manner. This is difficult for faculty to do and needs administrative support in order to occur.

If the leadership of the system does not take responsibility for system improvement, the chance of the system improving will not happen. Leaders improve the system, people work in the system, and everyone works to achieve the aim of the system. The principal and the faculty must look at the assessment of instruction, not only the results of instruction. If we improve the method, we improve the results!

Assessment-System Aim: Improve Instructional Methods and Achievement

1. Determine core values and standards that all agree need to be implemented.
2. Determine core curricular expectations at each level of the content areas.
3. Identify assessment criteria for each curricular expectation.
4. Identify observable indicators that demonstrate attainment of criteria at each level of student performance.

5. Determine the type of student-performance data to be gathered.
6. Determine the type of data analysis to evaluate student performance.
7. Determine the type of instructional-system data to be gathered.
8. Determine the type of data analysis to evaluate the instructional system.
9. Determine analyzed findings and recommendations for improvement.
10. Determine how recommendations are included in the school-improvement planning.

Process for Continual Improvement of the Academic Program

Student learning can be assessed in multiple ways. Student competencies can be demonstrated through project- and problem-based reports, videotape, digital files, electronic-portfolio files, and virtual strategies, as well as multiple other forms of testing data and teacher documentation. Therefore, the assessment strategies that are created to determine student competencies need to reflect these alternative strategies also.

Student assessment can demonstrate projects and knowledge through Internet links. Students need to be prepared for this type of assessment as well as through school-related activities. Of course, the traditional ways of assessing students are still valued and should continue when appropriate. Students need to demonstrate competencies through written work, oral reports, individual projects, group work, and many other assessment methods.

With the advent of new technologies, today's teachers and students have many options to demonstrate student learning. Together they can create many products that document student performance and can be used to improve instruction. As assessment of student learning becomes more informal and virtual, the teaching role in the student-teacher interaction becomes one of facilitator. Teacher as facilitator collaborates with students as they work together to plan and implement teaching and learning experiences.

GATHER DATA ON INSTRUCTIONAL STRATEGIES

When the faculty have determined student expectations at each academic level based on the required curriculum, then the faculty can determine criteria and observable indicators with respect to each student academic expectation. Now the task for the professional staff is to create assessment strategies that gather data on each of the instructional strategies being implemented in the teaching process. Once data are collected, they must be analyzed and assessed according to staff expectations and defined criteria. This concept of data analysis for continual system improvement is not commonly used at this time.

We are taught to gather data and evaluate the people who are implementing the instructional system, not the instructional system itself. This manner of thinking does not result in instructional-system improvement. It results in the faculty feeling the need to cheat, protect, close communication, not collaborate, and any number of other negative behaviors that take away from instructional-system improvement. If the leader understands the continual-improvement philosophy fully, the leader is evaluating the system and not the staff.

Data are only information and become knowledge when they are understood and interpreted as to how they might improve the system they represent. Once the principal and faculty are open to gathering and analyzing data with the purpose of improving the instructional system, all systems are go for risk taking with instructional strategies to improve teaching and learning.

This offers the faculty the opportunity to try new methods of instruction and test whether or not these methods are more effective. Then the concept of continual improvement of the instructional system is a reality. The aim is clear, and all are working to achieve the aim! The methods of instruction that teachers use are the keys to improving student performance. The faculty must be involved in instructional research to determine how the instructional methods are working with respect to student learning and how they can be improved.

1. Determine the instructional methods to be researched.
2. Determine observable indicators of these methods.

3. Determine criteria to assess these observable indicators.
4. Determine how to gather data on these methods.
5. Determine how the data are to be analyzed.
6. Determine how the findings will be used to improve the methods.
7. Determine how recommendations will be implemented.

GATHER DATA ON STUDENT CURRICULAR EXPECTATIONS

In addition to collecting data on the instructional system, the faculty collect data on student performance. Based on the curriculum criteria and observable indicators, assessment strategies are designed and implemented to gather information that can be analyzed to determine success of the academic program. It is critical to assess academic-program results in order to establish whether or not students are learning the required knowledge and meeting expectations.

The student-performance data demonstrate the effectiveness of the instructional system and the achievement of the curriculum system. Student-performance data show the result of all the hard work on the part of everyone in the school system. In order to assess data on student curricular expectations, the following steps are needed:

1. Clarify curricular expectations at each grade and course level for each content area.
2. Identify criteria for each student curricular expectation.
3. Identify observable indicators of acceptable performance for the criteria.
4. Determine the type of performance data to be gathered.
5. Determine the method of gathering the data.
6. Determine the method of analysis of the data.
7. Determine how the findings will be used to improve the system.
8. Determine how recommendations will be implemented.

These student-performance data are the result of the instructional system and many other variables in the school system. The faculty and administrative staff must determine what can be improved with respect to student performance from within the sphere of control that they are able to manage. Researching the student-performance data is important to achieving this goal.

ANALYZE ACADEMIC DATA USING STATISTICAL CONCEPTS

As the faculty plan to gather data on student performance, the type of data collected and the method of analysis are important to determine. Control charts have been used to analyze system data and are able to determine whether or not system improvements have occurred. Also, control charts can be used to determine common and special causes of system variation. Through the analysis of system data, the staff can determine the normal variation of the student results and if there is a special cause that needs to be investigated.

If there are no special causes to be investigated, the staff have to determine if the system-data results are acceptable. If the results are acceptable to the faculty, administrators, and community, then the process in place should remain in place. If the data results are not acceptable, the system process must be improved in order for positive change to occur. Only through system-data analysis is this determination possible (Wheeler 1992).

If special causes of variation occur, the system is not predictable unless these special causes are removed. Only through the investigation of the system is knowledge gained to remove these causes. After these special causes are removed, the professional staff are able to understand the true output capacity of the present system. Then the faculty can determine whether intervention into the system is necessary or not. As time goes on, additional data can be collected and analyzed against previous data, and evaluations and recommendations are possible for system improvement (Wheeler 1993). Please review chapter 2 for control-chart analysis.

The figure 6.1 data were collected from all fifth-grade students who were given a reading-inventory assessment. Each student was assessed by a reading specialist, and the scores of each student are grouped by reading level for the class of 126 students (from the chart on p. 84 [Warwick 1995]).

These student reading–assessment data do not tell us anything about whether the variance is meaningful or not. However, by running a

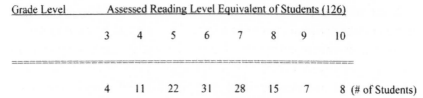

Grade Level	Assessed Reading Level Equivalent of Students (126)							
	3	4	5	6	7	8	9	10
	4	11	22	31	28	15	7	8 (# of Students)

Figure 6.1. Individual-Student Reading-Level Equivalents

control chart of these data, one can understand this system statistically and decide additional action to be taken to assist certain students and improve this system.

In figure 6.2, the fifth-grade reading-inventory assessments show the scores of 126 students tested in September of the school year. These data show the mean (Process Center Line [PCL]) to be a 6.5 reading level with an upper control limit of 9.2 and a lower control limit of 3.8. Common causes of variation are within the control limits, and special causes of variation are outside of the control limits. In this chart, ten students are above the upper control limit, and four students are below the lower control limit. When data go beyond the control limits, they must be investigated to determine whether they represent special cases that need to be addressed.

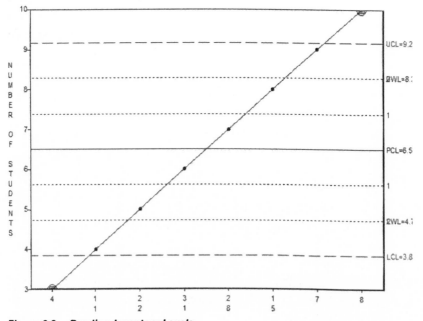

Figure 6.2. Reading-Inventory Levels

In the situation in which eighth-grade students are reading at level ten, these are wonderful situations and special causes that do need to be addressed with enrichment options if the students wish. Also, one may wish to investigate these students to determine whether or not there is any evidence of common instructional strategies that may be helpful for other students in the future. In the case of the four students who are below the lower control limit, these students are in need of special attention and need to have their level of instruction reassessed. The reassessment data may determine the need for individual tutorial interventions.

The reading-score variation of the studies falling on or within the control limits is normal and part of the system itself, and, if satisfactory to the staff, this reading program is acceptable for the general student population. If the scores of these students are not acceptable to the staff, planning an intervention to improve the instructional system is in order.

Different types of data can be accessed through different types of control charts. Quantitative and qualitative data can be analyzed through the use of various charts. As different types of instructional interventions are introduced into the system, the faculty can determine whether or not the intervention improves the results. It is through this process of instructional analysis that continual improvement of the instructional system is achieved. As the methods of instruction improve, student achievement improves. The only way to know this information about a system is to do control chart–data analysis (Warwick 1995, chaps. 3 and 5).

1. Identify the type of data to be collected.
2. Determine the method of data gathering.
3. Determine the type of data analysis.
4. Gather the data.
5. Run the control chart.
6. Analyze the control chart.
7. Draw conclusions from the data analysis.
8. Recommend improvements based on the conclusion.

Control-chart analysis is the only way one can tell how the system is operating. Also, this analysis helps educators understand the capacity of the system and if one is satisfied with system results. Normal-distribution statistical analysis will not give you this type of data analysis. We must be able to analyze system data, not just be able to describe it. Analysis of control-chart data helps us understand system capacity and moves us toward the possibility of system improvement (QualityAmerica, 2014). Please review control-chart analysis in chapter 1.

SHARE ACADEMIC DATA AND ANALYSIS
WITH ALL PROFESSIONAL STAFF

In order for the faculty to benefit from the data gathered from instructional strategies and student performance, the data need to be shared with other family members. Sharing data with the faculty is needed for future planning and creating improvement strategies. As each teacher in the school shares data, curricular expectations are reviewed as to their effectiveness and appropriateness for this level.

Not only are the data shared with respect to student results, data with respect to instructional methods are shared and discussed. Through sharing of this data, the staff become aware of areas most needing improvement. Also, these shared data provide vital information and set targets for the future school-improvement planning team. Assessment steps that allow for this analysis and sharing are as follows:

1. Instructional teams analyze data from their instructional methods and student-performance results.
2. Instructional teams draw conclusions from their findings.
3. Instructional teams synthesize recommendations from conclusions.
4. Each instructional team reports conclusions and recommendations to building instructional-improvement team.
5. Building instructional-improvement team reports all conclusions and recommendations to the entire faculty.
6. Instructional teams discuss the building instructional-improvement team's report of all conclusions and recommendations.
7. Instructional teams make final recommendations to the building instructional-improvement team.
8. Building instructional-improvement team recommends to the faculty the priorities to be addressed for the next academic year.
9. All faculty give feedback to the recommendations.

10. Revisions of the recommendations are addressed if needed.
11. Recommendations are submitted into the school-improvement planning process for inclusion in next year's plan.

Data-based decisions with respect to the instructional system are essential to the improvement process of the academic program. The principal and faculty must continue to study the instructional system and improve these methods in order to meet the needs of the student body. Once the faculty are involved in instructional research, the findings from their studies must be shared with all staff, and results must be implemented to improve the system.

1. Determine instructional methods to be researched.
2. Determine research design.
3. Implement research design.
4. Determine findings.
5. Share findings with all faculty.
6. Determine changes to be made.
7. Implement improvements.

SHARE ACADEMIC DATA WITH COMMUNITY PARTNERS

When student academic data are shared with the community, strategies for improvement are discussed and planned for the next school-improvement cycle. The community is a partner in the improvement process and needs to understand the instructional system and the results coming from that system. Through this process of sharing, the faculty and community build mutual respect and agree on future priorities in the academic program. This is the method by which support for the academic program is achieved within the community. With community support, the school can achieve its goals; without community support, the school cannot achieve its goals.

The community is the school's greatest partner, and the school needs the community's support to continually improve all aspects of the academic program. As the recommendations for instructional improvement come to the building-leadership team, the recommendations are shared with the parents and other community members. Also, they are invited to small-group discussions with the staff. The sharing process includes the following steps:

1. Each instructional team reports conclusions and recommendations to building instructional-improvement team.
2. Building-leadership team reports conclusions and recommendations to the entire faculty.
3. Instructional teams discuss the building-leadership team's report.
4. Instructional teams make final recommendations to the building instructional-improvement team.
5. Building-leadership team recommends to the faculty the priorities to be addressed for the next academic year.
6. All faculty give feedback to the recommendations.
7. Parents and community members are invited to discuss recommendations at the instructional team level in small groups.
8. Revisions of the recommendations are addressed if needed.
9. Recommendations are submitted into the school-improvement planning process for inclusion in next year's plan.

It is important that the community be informed and involved in the instructional-change process. Instructional improvements that are going to be recommended to the school-improvement planning process need to be shared and discussed with the community members before the changes are implemented. This type of respect for community input builds trust and support for the educational programs and the entire school.

INVOLVE COMMUNITY PARTNERS IN THE SCHOOL-IMPROVEMENT PROCESS

The school-improvement planning process includes the members of the community in order to determine and affirm the goals of the school. Community members are included in meetings to discuss academic and instructional-process findings and future strategies for improvement. Collaboration and cooperation among different elements of the community are critical for the success of the schooling process in any community.

One of the best ways to build support is to involve community members in the school-improvement planning process. One suggestion might be to create a parent/community advisory team that meets with the building instructional-improvement team to discuss the instructional-improvement recommendations before the final school-improvement plan is written. This would allow for community input and feedback within the formal process. The building instructional-improvement team recommends to the faculty the priorities to be addressed for the next academic year.

1. All faculty give feedback to the recommendations.
2. Parents and community members are invited to discuss recommendations at the instructional-team level in small groups.
3. Revisions of the recommendations are addressed if needed.
4. Recommendations are submitted into the school-improvement planning-process team for inclusion in next year's plan.
5. Parent/community advisory team discusses recommendations and gives feedback to the school-improvement planning-process team.
6. Building instructional-improvement team writes final school-improvement plan for the next academic year.

Community support is the key to an effective academic program, and any way the community members can contribute to the improvement of the program should be encouraged. Truly, it takes the whole community to educate the children.

RECOMMENDATIONS TO REVISE THE SCHOOL-IMPROVEMENT PLAN

Once the data from the student academic results are analyzed and discussed, the goal of the school-improvement planning team is to revise the school-improvement plan for the following school year. The leadership team determines new priorities, and these are shared with all components of the school community. These priorities become the driving force for the faculty professional-development programs for the next school year. Also, these priorities drive the budget allocations with respect to instructional materials and instructional-improvement strategies to be implemented.

The philosophy of continual improvement becomes the aim of the professional staff, and the school-improvement planning process becomes a way of life. Everyone wins in this system, and the joy of learning and teaching is possible! In addition to using the recommendations for the new school-improvement plan, the professional staff use this information to design the professional-development program for the next school year. This has implications for the budget and needs to be addressed in budget projections for the next year.

1. Recommendations go to the school-improvement planning team.
2. Allocation for professional development is set aside for recommendations to be implemented in the coming academic year.
3. Recommendations are incorporated into the new school-improvement plan.
4. Research designs are planned for the instructional innovations to assess and improve the instructional system.

ASSESSMENT-SYSTEM SURVEY

5.0   Assessment System

    5.1   *Professional staff understand assessment is the evaluation of the instruction system.* The staff understand that assessment is critical to the continual improvement of instruction, which in turn improves the student-learning opportunities. The assessment system gathers and analyzes data and recommends strategies to improve instruction.

        1   2   3   4   5   6   7   8   9

    5.2   *Professional staff use various strategies to assess student learning.* Student learning is assessed through various strategies. Some of the strategies teachers use to assess student performance are paper-and-pencil tests, oral reports, written reports, individual projects, team projects, community work, and other contract agreements. The student portfolio includes multiple assessment data to give a diverse perspective of the student's ability and capacity.

1   2   3   4   5   6   7   8   9

5.3   *Professional staff gather data on instructional strategies.*
Staff cooperate to gather and analyze data on instructional strategies. Analyzing instructional-strategy data leads to investigating the relationship between instructional strategies and student learning. Studying this relationship may lead to revising instruction to improve student learning and performance.

1   2   3   4   5   6   7   8   9

5.4   *Professional staff gather data on student curricular performance.* Student academic-performance data are gathered and analyzed to assess the results of the instructional program. This data analysis allows the faculty to judge if the instructional system is improving and meeting academic expectations. This assessment is critical to the continual improvement of the entire academic program and is the lifeblood of the schooling process.

1   2   3   4   5   6   7   8   9

5.5   *Professional staff analyze academic data using statistical-analysis concepts.* Student-performance data are analyzed using statistical concepts. This analysis enables the staff to understand the system of instruction with respect to common causes of variation and special causes of variation. Common variation always exists within the system because it is built into the system itself. When only common causes of variation exist in the system, past system performance can predict future behavior. Special variation is not part of the normal process and causes the process to be unpredictable. When special variation exists, it is excessive and can be assigned to a specific cause. Statistical analysis of data allows the staff to understand these types of variations in order to predict and improve instructional strategies and student performance.

1   2   3   4   5   6   7   8   9

5.6   *Professional staff share academic analysis and findings with all faculty.* After data are gathered and analyzed, the staff share their findings with the entire staff to enable additional discussion and improvement of instruction. Everyone on the faculty is working on the instructional system to improve it. Unless everyone has knowledge of the data analysis and findings, it is not possible to be part of the improvement process.

1   2   3   4   5   6   7   8   9

5.7   *Professional staff use academic findings to improve instructional strategies.* If the findings from the data analysis suggest better instructional strategies with respect to specific student-academic expectations, the faculty implement these changes. However, if the findings from the data analysis determine that certain instructional practices are not productive, they need to be discontinued. In either case, the aim is to continually improve the instructional system through data-based analysis.

1   2   3   4   5   6   7   8   9

5.8   *Professional staff share academic findings with their community partners.* The staff continually provide school community members with updates on academic progress with respect to changes in the instructional strategies and student-performance results.

1   2   3   4   5   6   7   8   9

5.9   *Professional staff involve community partners in the school-improvement process.* The staff not only share the academic data, analysis, and findings with community members, they also invite community partners to discuss future school academic priorities and concerns. This relationship with the community partners is continual and supports a learning community spirit. Without community support for the academic-improvement process and involvement in the school academic-improvement planning process, neither of these efforts can be successful or effective.

1   2   3   4   5   6   7   8   9

5.10   *Professional staff use recommendations to revise the school-improvement plan.* Based on the recommendations from the school-improvement process, priorities are identified and included in the future school-improvement plan. Priorities are stated in terms of staff-development strategies that help staff improve student learning and performance with respect to these priorities.

1   2   3   4   5   6   7   8   9

CHAPTER 7

Professional Behaviors and Values

System: Leader deciding what matters and legacy
System aim: Self-growth
Methodology: Forgiveness, humility, caring for others, and staying the
course

As many of you have studied and analyzed different philosophies, theories, leadership styles, and authors' ideas, you start to discern concepts and practices that are acceptable to you and build them into your beliefs and behaviors. The people I've studied who have shaped my thinking and behavior over the years are John Goodlad, Ken Blanchard, and W. Edwards Deming.

Along the way, others have guided me through situations and challenges that have been valuable and caused heartfelt reflections. However, when I reflect on behaviors, beliefs, and values applied to the educational profession and personal life, these three men stand above all others and are worthy of study.

John Goodlad led a project known as *individually guided education* supported by the Charles F. Kettering Foundation in the late 1960s. The aim of this project was to create a new model for schooling by introducing multiage, multigrade, integrated team staffing and linked decision making as basic operations within the school and district.

As educators reflect on the *multiunit-school* concept of the late 1960s and '70s, many elements that characterized this system are relevant today, such as levels of communication, integrated-curriculum units, multiage grouping of students, multigrade integration for instruction, criterion-reference assessment, objective-based performance learning, and integrated-content teaching teams. Many of these ideas are being integrated into our school today as thematic units of study and project- and problem-based learning systems.

Ken Blanchard introduced the idea of *situational leadership*, which asks leaders to analyze each situation when interacting with a col- league. Situational leadership asks the leader to assess the competence and commitment of the task in order to interact appropriately about the task with the follower. The task analysis with respect to competence and commitment is a wonderful process for a leader to assess the per- son's knowledge and attitude with respect to performing a task.

Through this task analysis, a leader can decide if the follower, with respect to a given task, is to be directed, coached, supported, or del- egated with respect to implementing the task at hand. This process of analysis respects the leader and follower in a mutual relationship and values both parties.

W. Edwards Deming opened the world of understanding systems and the concept of continual improvement. Also, by using some basic statistical tools, one can start to improve any process, and system. If a process is improved, the system results are improved. The greatest mind-opening concept that Dr. Deming contributed to leadership is the idea of working on the system and not demeaning the people in the system. Understanding the system and knowing how to improve it is the challenge that can help leaders address and collaborate with others to assist in doing so.

Too often leaders blame others when something goes wrong instead of analyzing the system and process, integrating everyone in the im- provement decision-making process and using basic statistical tools to analyze and solve the problem. If you wish to deepen and expand your leadership competencies, studying these ideas can add great breadth and depth to your knowledge and understanding of what leaders need to bring to the table to be effective.

One concept I heard over and over from these teachers was that "power not used is often abused." One comes to understand this upon listening to what Ken Blanchard said—that "Leaders set the goals; followers implement the goals!" At first, one may not agree and react negatively to this phrase, but as one understands more deeply what this means, its truth becomes evident. This does not mean others cannot be involved in discussion and analysis of ideas but, rather, that in the last analysis the leader must make the decision and is responsible for setting goals. After a leader understands this, it's easy to agree with Blanchard.

The statement does not mean that a leader dictates goals, demands goals, or does not consider others in the goal-setting process; rather the leader does decide what goals are selected to implement. This is the leader's responsibility. W. Edwards Deming would often say, "If the leader is not willing to improve the system, who else is going to do it?" The leader is the only one in the position to lead! That is the leader's job! Once the leader decides to lead, everyone becomes a member of the leadership team.

AIMING TO CONTINUALLY IMPROVE
THE INSTRUCTIONAL PROCESS

1. Create constancy of purpose toward improvement of the instructional process with the aim of enhancing continual growth in knowledge and joy in learning to improve self-development and the society in which we live.[1]

   1.1   Leaders clarify and communicate the school aim throughout the school and community.

   1.2   Leaders create a collaborative environment in which everyone works together to achieve the aim of the school.

2. Adopt this new philosophy! Leaders must awaken to the challenge, learn their responsibilities, and accept their role of leadership for change.

   2.1   Leaders are responsible for learning a new philosophy characterized by cooperation and collaboration. Commit to continual improvement!

   2.2   Leaders create open communication and cooperation between people at all levels of the system through horizontally and vertically integrated teams.

3. Cease dependency on mass inspection to achieve quality (continual improvement). Eliminate the need for inspection on a mass basis by building continual improvement into the implementation of the instructional process.

   3.1   Criterion-referenced assessment should be the standard procedure for analyzing student performance. Grading and ranking do not assure learning and improvement of instruction. Learning opportunities are independent of age or grade-level grouping.

   3.2   Student feedback on the instructional process should be built into the system.

4. Cease the practice of awarding contracts on the basis of price. Instead, minimize total cost and integrate management and learning systems utilizing varied organizational and community resources. Build trust and work with single suppliers to benefit the system.

   4.1   Cooperate with other community agencies on coordinating educational programs and cost projections for greater purchasing power.

   4.2   Maximize system cost-effectiveness by integrating curricular goals, instructional planning, and material purchasing.

5. Improve constantly and forever the system of management of the school services, and decrease managerial and instructional costs. Go upstream to prevent errors and waste and improve the system.

   5.1   Leaders educate the staff with basic statistical skill, control-chart analysis, knowledge of common and special causes of variation, and the means of determining where the system needs improvement.

   5.2   Implement the *plan-do-study-act* cycle. Start with data gathering; then analyze the data, determine the needs, identify causes of deficiencies, identify solutions, make recommendations, and design interventions for improvement. Continue the cycle.

6. Continually train on the critical elements of the instructional process.

   6.1   Provide expert training in how to gather and analyze information and software training for statistical-data analysis!

   6.2   Use learning-style assessment and variable instructional strategies to meet and expand various student-learning styles.

7. Leadership creates an environment that enables improvement and change by providing systems of cooperation and collaboration through communication systems and through teaching and implementing the continual-improvement philosophy in the workplace through words and deeds.

   7.1   Create levels of communication within the system for horizontal and vertical information flow and input for decision making.

   7.2   Work on improving the systems, not blaming the people! Understand common and special causes for variation, and respond appropriately.

8. Leaders drive out fear and encourage communication. Everyone works together to achieve the aim. Leaders remove conditions that cause fear of learning, such as competition, reprisal, ridicule, and embarrassment.

   8.1   Build trust! The aim is to create an atmosphere in which risk can be taken, mistakes can be made, and experimentation is encouraged without reprisal.

   8.2   Everyone wins when the instructional process is improved!

9. Break down barriers between all units.

   9.1   Create horizontal and vertical linkage between and among grade levels, academic departments, administrative departments, schools, and various systems.

   9.2   Improving instruction is a team effort and a team process: everyone wins!

10. Leaders eliminate slogans and targets that create the pressure to do quality work without the means to do so. Unrealistic expectations increase adversarial relationships and stress the system and everyone in it. These ideas lower achievement in the system.

    10.1   Quotas do not create quality! Educating people to implement improved systems creates quality.

    10.2   Educating people on system understanding and using tools to continually improve the system provide a path to success. Educating people on methods of improving the instructional process determines academic achievement.

11. Leaders implement assessment strategies so students can affirm learning and predict their readiness for future instruction and enable future learning. Leaders eliminate managing by objectives, managing by results, and managing by numbers and numerical goals. Leaders continually improve systems, and the results take care of themselves.

    11.1   Teach students how to think at higher levels of cognition. Expect and create opportunities for higher-level thinking and decision making. Determine expected student-learning outcomes and criterion-referenced assessments to measure student academic progress and achievement.

    11.2   Use standardized-assessment systems for data gathering and trend analysis but never for individual student assessment. Analysis of trends can be used to determine needs for improvement, and samplings of large populations should be considered to do this, not assessing everyone (massive standardized assessment).

    11.3   Educate staff on basic statistical strategies to improve instructional process and not to evaluate staff.

    11.4   Base professional advancement on the ability to improve systems and to use knowledge consistent with improving system quality.

12. Remove barriers that keep pride of workmanship from staff and students.

12.1 Abolish staff-rating systems, and build collaborative teacher-support groups, mentoring systems, and professional-growth systems for instructional excellence.

12.2 Reward and recognize teachers for implementing outstanding improvements in instruction and program improvement. Create an opportunity for these teachers to mentor others.

13. Create a program of continual professional-staff development.

13.1 Embrace a life-long learning model for all to see and affirm.

13.2 Gain new knowledge, and grow professionally.

14. Transform the schooling organization and the learning process for everyone. Quality instruction is the aim for everyone!

14.1 Leaders are responsible for professional growth of all the people in the system.

14.2 Leaders are responsible for designing, developing, and encouraging cooperation and collaboration throughout the educational system.

14.3 Leaders provide visions, aims, and goals: staff and students implement them, and all gain. The entire community of learners cooperates, collaborates, and wins!

CHALLENGE FOR LEADERS: TRANSFORMING SELF AND OTHERS

We all come from different backgrounds, but effective leaders demonstrate common traits and abilities that add value to any organization of which they are a part. Some general traits of effective leaders follow:

1. *An effective leader sees clearly.* Leaders understand that each school is a unit of change. The mission is continual improvement of each system to enable each person to grow and prepare for each person's next move and advance in learning to make the move.

2. *An effective leader is a team player.* Create teams of people at all levels in the organization, and integrate their communication

systems to allow continual improvement of every system to achieve the aim of the school. Improvement is a team effort; it cannot be achieved individually!

3. *An effective leader offers genuine support.* Leaders are constantly providing support and encouragement to the staff. Also, the leader helps staff to acquire needed materials and other resources to implement the instructional systems to benefit the students. The leader is a staff cheerleader!

4. *An effective leader relies on statistical data.* Leaders teach the staff how to use statistical data–analysis tools to determine areas needing improvement and discuss strategies for improvement. Leaders must know the difference between common and special causes of variation and must not mislead the staff and waste time on trying to improve the wrong things.

CONCEPTS AND VALUES TO CHALLENGE AND DIRECT YOUR LEADERSHIP THINKING AND ACTION

1. *Commit to a common purpose.* A leader must create a common purpose for teamwork to have a chance in any aspect of life, be it at home or in the workplace.

2. *Every person is of equal value, period.* Everyone should have a voice in the process of decision making and contribute to the goals of the unit of which they are a part. Everyone may not get his or her way on an issue, but each person had an opportunity to participate in the process.

3. *Good decisions are based on good information and collaborative analysis of this information.* Data and analysis must be shared with all who are involved in the decision-making process so everyone knows why the decision is being made. All may not agree with the final decision; however, they will all know why the decision had to be made.

4. *We are human and make mistakes.* Improve future actions, support the players, and learn from the mistake. Work on improving the process, lead with knowledge and understanding, and develop the people to improve the process.

5. *Professional development is essential to improvement and is forever ongoing.* As each year goes by, new knowledge and challenges are in front of us. Each member of the professional staff must face them, study them, learn from them, and then address them.

6. *Higher cognitive processes are taught and do not automatically develop when one grows older.* Each person can learn to think more critically, and the mind must be challenged to develop higher levels of mental processes—such as application, analysis, evaluation, and synthesis.

7. *Foster a joy of learning; remove the fear of offering new ways of thinking and problem solving.* Implement systems where people are encouraged to participate, and get involved in improving the teaching and learning strategies.

8. *Be a team player!* No one can do it alone. A leader needs to lead someone. Team leaders lead by example and support the team's achieving its aims. Leaders consult team members and involve them in all aspects of their planning and actions to complete the mission; however, the leader needs to make decisions, and the team implements them.

9. *Leaders are accountable for the process and performance of the system they are leading.* At the end of the day, the leader must reflect on the goals, implementations, results, and overall operations of any organization and answer for its performance.

10. *Aim to leave things better than when we entered!* We are part of a process of growth and development, and we need to advance the processes so others can take over and continue to improve them. Each of us is here but a moment in time—though a critical and valuable moment!

NOTE

1. These principles are based on Dr. Deming's fourteen points (Warwick 1995, chap. 10).

School Academic-Systems Improvement Survey

School academic-systems improvement is based on the continual-improvement philosophy. Continual improvement requires understanding how systems determine performance and how collaboration is essential for school-systems improvement. The school academic-improvement systems clarify the aims of each system and integrate the following systems: system structures and elements, communication, curriculum, instruction, and assessment. *System structures and elements* defines and explains a system and its characteristics of a system. The *communication system* establishes a network that facilitates collaboration and optimization of system components. The *curriculum system* clarifies and aligns student expectations throughout the schooling process. The *instruction system* determines the methods and structures through which students engage the curriculum. The *assessment system* gathers and analyzes data to evaluate instructional-strategy effectiveness and student academic achievement. This philosophy requires a new way of thinking about academic improvement for each and every teacher and student to win.

SCHOOL SURVEY–RESPONSE DIRECTIONS

The survey consists of fifty items and asks you to determine whether or not each item is present in your working environment. Also, it is very important that you not judge each item as good or bad, desirable or undesirable, but, rather, that you determine *to what degree the item is present in your work environment*. The range of choices is 1 through 9: (1) indicating *never present* and (9) indicating *always present*.

Never	About Half	Always

————————————————————————————

1   2   3   4   5   6   7   8   9

Figure A.1.   Professional Staff Perception of Best Practice Implementation

Please indicate the number that reflects your perception of each item present in your work environment at this time.

1.0   System Structures and Elements

   1.1   *Professional staff understand the concept of* system. A *system* is defined as a series of components that work together within an organization for the purpose (*aim*) of the organization. Each component in a system works together to benefit other components in a system and to achieve the aim of the total system. (In the organizational system, components such as time schedule, instructional teams, team planning time, curriculum design, and classroom organization are key components.) Three key elements in understanding a system are defining the system, clarifying the purpose of the system, and determining by what method the purpose will be achieved in the system.

   1   2   3   4   5   6   7   8   9

   1.2   *Professional staff identify key system components.* Each major system component and its function are identified. (One component of the school organizational system is the *communication structure and process* for decision making.) Without identification, the component and its relationship to other components are not clear and the system is not effective.

   1   2   3   4   5   6   7   8   9

   1.3   *Professional staff state system purposes.* The system purpose or aim gives meaning to the integration of all components. If the purpose or aim of the system is not stated clearly, each component cannot perform its function as it serves the system.

1   2   3   4   5   6   7   8   9

1.4   *Professional staff clarify system purposes.* Once the system purpose or aim is stated, the words need to be clarified or defined so everyone understands the statement. Everyone working on the system has to have the same understanding of the purpose of the system.

1   2   3   4   5   6   7   8   9

1.5   *Professional staff communicate system purposes.* Once the system purpose or aim is stated and clarified, the purpose or aim is communicated in writing to all partners within the system. The purpose is clearly stated so all members working on the system maintain a clear and constant focus.

1   2   3   4   5   6   7   8   9

1.6   *Professional staff identify methods to achieve system purposes.* Methods are the means by which the purpose of the system is achieved. Instructional strategies, for example, are the methods teachers use to achieve the purpose of student learning.

1   2   3   4   5   6   7   8   9

1.7   *Professional staff assess system purposes.* Gathering data on specific purpose indicators is the means by which the system is assessed. Without gathering data on key elements of the system, the staff are not able to evaluate the system with respect to process improvement and system results. If a specific system strategy is implemented, data on this strategy as well as system performance using this strategy need to be gathered.

1   2   3   4   5   6   7   8   9

1.8   *Professional staff statistically analyze system data.* Data are gathered on system indicators (*criteria*) identified by the staff, such as effective decision making, team collaboration, and statistical-data analysis. System statistical analysis is used to identify data trends and causes of variation.

1   2   3   4   5   6   7   8   9

1.9   *Professional staff identify trends based on the data.* The staff recognize academic trends based on the data analysis. These trends are discussed with respect to implications for improvement.

1   2   3   4   5   6   7   8   9

1.10   *Professional staff implement improvement strategies.* The staff implement revised strategies based on the academic organizational-improvement trends supported by the data analysis. Improvement is judged on moving the system population in the direction of the system purpose or aim.

1   2   3   4   5   6   7   8   9

2.0   Communication System

2.1   *Professional staff respect the philosophy of continual improvement through its cooperative efforts to achieve academic improvement.* This philosophy enables staff members to work together for their mutual benefit and for the improvement of the academic program. In order to cooperate, staff are aware of information on issues to make informed decisions. Cooperation is demonstrated through mutual trust and respect for all parties to gain and for no party to gain at the expense of another. Staff work within an academic system, leaders work on the academic system, and everyone works toward continual improvement of the academic system to achieve the purpose of student learning.

1   2   3   4   5   6   7   8   9

2.2   *Professional staff participate in the school academic-improvement planning process.* Staff are informed of the student-performance data at each grade or course level in the school. Based on the data analysis, the staff recommend curricular priorities and suggest strategies for improvement to be stated in the academic school-improvement plan.

    1   2   3   4   5   6   7   8   9

2.3   *Professional staff and others write the academic school-improvement plan.* The staff work together to write the academic school-improvement plan:

    1.0   Academic philosophy (mission and beliefs)
    2.0   Academic aims (purpose and objectives)
    3.0   Academic-data analysis (local and national assessments)
    4.0   Academic priorities (curriculum trends and analysis)
    5.0   Improvement strategies (improvement summary)
    6.0   Assessment of strategies (performance summary)
    7.0   Community update (communication plan)

    1   2   3   4   5   6   7   8   9

2.4   *Administrator organizes staff into instructional teams.* An administrator organizes the staff into grade-level teams (first grade), multidisciplinary teams (sixth-grade content areas), multigrade-level teams (first, second, third grade), or content-area teams (high school math). These instructional teams are organized to integrate content and methodology to enhance student learning.

    1   2   3   4   5   6   7   8   9

2.5   *Administrator schedules common planning time during the school day for instructional teams.* Instructional teams have common planning time for professional collaboration.

This time is used for planning curricular units, designing instructional strategies, designing assessment methods, and continually improving the academic system.

1   2   3   4   5   6   7   8   9

2.6   *Instructional teams use consensus methods to make decisions. Consensus decision making* is defined as each person accepting the decision. Agreement with the decision is not critical; however, willingness to go along with the decision *is* critical. If a person is not able to come to this level of acceptance, the discussion must continue until consensus is reached.

1   2   3   4   5   6   7   8   9

2.7   *Administrators and teachers create an agenda for the building-leadership team meetings.* The administrators and teachers create an agenda. The agenda is written and shared with instructional teams prior to the meeting, and no item is added to the agenda after it is shared with the instructional teams. If new agenda items are identified after the agenda has gone out, the new items go on the next agenda.

1   2   3   4   5   6   7   8   9

2.8   *Administrator meets with instructional-team leaders weekly to address academic improvement.* Instructional-team leaders represent the instructional team. These representatives meet with an administrator weekly to discuss various issues for improvement with respect to academic organization, communication, curriculum, instruction, and assessment improvements.

1   2   3   4   5   6   7   8   9

2.9   *Instructional teams receive written minutes of the building-team leadership meetings.* Written minutes are shared with

each member the next day. The minutes contain each
agenda item, the decision, and the rationale.

1   2   3   4   5   6   7   8   9

2.10   *Instructional team leaders review building-leadership
meeting minutes with team members.* Team leaders clarify and discuss the building-leadership meeting minutes
with team members.

1   2   3   4   5   6   7   8   9

3.0   Curriculum System

3.1   *Professional staff understand the process of curriculum alignment.* The process of the curriculum alignment
reflects vertical and horizontal networks that address
student-learning needs and expectations. (Vertical networks coordinate content-area expectations in sequential
order from prekindergarten through twelfth grade, math
sequence from prekindergarten through twelfth grade).
Horizontal networks integrate content-area expectations
through all content areas by grade level (math, science, social studies, language arts, art, music, etc.). The alignment
process determines the sequence and scope of the curriculum and is the framework for the instructional system.

1   2   3   4   5   6   7   8   9

3.2   *Professional staff align curricular expectations horizontally.* Curricular expectations are integrated across a
grade level with respect to content areas. This content integration allows students to synthesize their knowledge.
Many students are not able to integrate information unless it is presented in a manner that relates these different
perspectives together. Knowledge from different content
areas at the same level can be aligned to enhance student
integration of the material.

1   2   3   4   5   6   7   8   9

3.3   *Professional staff align curricular expectations verti-cally.* Curricular expectations are sequenced throughout the academic program to build and support each other. The faculty analyze each level of expectations to assure that they build upon previous levels. Each academic grade or course blends with the one before and after, creating a flow of expectations that enhances student learning.

    1   2   3   4   5   6   7   8   9

3.4   *Professional staff integrate state academic standards into curricular expectations to determine grade- and course-level student expectations.* District grade- and course-level curricular expectations are aligned and state academic standards integrated to determine student aca-demic expectations at each level in the district academic program. Student academic expectations may exceed state standards, which are viewed as basic at each level. District and school curricula are the blueprint for student learning. The state standards are the minimum guidelines that must be addressed within the school curriculum

    1   2   3   4   5   6   7   8   9

3.5   *Professional staff write grade- and course-level expec-tations relating and integrating various content areas of study.* The staff develop and write units of study that incorporate student academic expectations from different content areas of study. An example of relating content ar-eas with respect to the study of the environment is graph-ing population growth in mathematics, reading about cul-ture in language arts and social sciences, and examining geological formations in science. The unit of study would relate this information in a manner that would enable stu-dents to understand the interrelationships of this material.

    1   2   3   4   5   6   7   8   9

3.6   *Professional staff integrate levels of critical thinking within content areas of study.* As the unit of study is developed, each of the cognitive levels of critical thinking is designed into the unit. Activities based on the unit content are designed to require each student to know, comprehend, apply, analyze, synthesize, and evaluate information within the area of study.

    1   2   3   4   5   6   7   8   9

3.7   *Professional staff organize curriculum sequence to enhance student learning.* Curricular expectations are sequenced horizontally and vertically within and across content areas to enable students to understand interrelationships and draw larger meaning from their study. The sequence of learning knowledge may enhance student ability to understand and grow academically. Based on research and experience, the faculty sequence the curriculum in a manner most beneficial to each student's learning style and capacity.

    1   2   3   4   5   6   7   8   9

3.8   *Professional staff organize curriculum scope to enhance student learning.* The depth of each curricular expectation is designed into the units of study to enable each student to gain new knowledge based on previously learned information. As students move from learning unit to learning unit, grade level to grade level, school to school, the curriculum flows in a manner that builds student knowledge and understanding.

    1   2   3   4   5   6   7   8   9

3.9   *Professional staff write criteria for each curricular expectation.* Criteria for each curricular expectation are written to communicate to the faculty and students the level of knowledge needed to demonstrate acceptable evidence of student learning. Criteria are used to assess the instructional process and student performance on critical expectations. Unless criteria are clear, the staff are not able to understand whether or not students are learning and the instructional process is achieving its aim.

1   2   3   4   5   6   7   8   9

3.10   *Professional staff write observable indicators for criteria to determine student performance with respect to each student-learning expectation.* Each criterion needs specific observable indicators to identify student-learned knowledge. These indicators are the basis for data gathering and analysis, which allows for continual instructional and academic improvement. The improvement process is totally dependent on this issue being addressed and implemented. If it is not implemented, the entire continual-improvement philosophy is undermined and the continual-improvement process will fail.

1   2   3   4   5   6   7   8   9

4.0   Instruction System

4.1   *Professional staff understand instruction is the method to achieve academic improvement.* Instruction is the method teachers use to stimulate student interest and enhance learning. Through various instructional strategies, teachers create an environment in which student learning comes alive. Instruction is the means by which the teacher leads the student to achieve the academic expectations stated in the school curriculum. Instruction is the means to the academic aim, which is student learning. Continual improvement of instruction is the method by which continual improvement of student learning is achieved.

1   2   3   4   5   6   7   8   9

4.2   *Teachers plan the instructional lessons.* The faculty plan instructional lessons to facilitate student learning through classroom activities. Lessons consist of objectives, teaching strategies, guided student practice, reteaching strategies if needed, follow-up activities, and student products meeting previously established criteria to assure learning.

1   2   3   4   5   6   7   8   9

4.3   *Teachers integrate content areas in the learning lesson when possible.* Content-area integration enables students to synthesize information and view issues from multiple perspectives. Often this content integration can be accomplished through a thematic unit. The aim is to relate different areas of knowledge in such a manner as to allow the student to integrate ideas and to understand these relationships.

1   2   3   4   5   6   7   8   9

4.4   *Teachers organize the environment for learning.* Classroom organization can facilitate different types of learning. Different structures enhance different modes of instruction (theater seating for large-group lecture, table groupings for small-group discussion, and individual learning stations for independent study). If the learning environment is structured for different learning styles, students can use multiple opportunities to learn the same information. Also, a student may use his or her primary learning style to learn difficult material and reinforce learning through a secondary style. Some students may enjoy learning new knowledge through various learning styles and welcome the options made available within the environment.

1   2   3   4   5   6   7   8   9

4.5   *Teachers provide instructional materials appropriate for various student needs.* Teachers provide appropriate materials for student reading levels, motor abilities, hearing capacities, physical skills, and many other needs. As diversity increases in the student body, alternative materials to meet these diverse student needs are essential. Instructional materials of different modes and levels are required in every instructional setting. One cannot know which type of instructional material is most helpful for any student at any given time.

1   2   3   4   5   6   7   8   9

4.6   *Teachers clarify student-learning expectations for the instructional lesson.* Teachers clarify student-learning expectations at the beginning of each lesson. These expectations are determined by the curriculum system and are stated in the units of study developed by the faculty. Students should be aware of the academic expectations in advance to give direction and purpose to the learning experience. In addition to the students, parents and other interested parties may wish to know student academic expectations, and this information can be made available when requested.

1   2   3   4   5   6   7   8   9

4.7   *Teachers implement strategies to facilitate student activities for each cognitive level.* Each teacher implements instructional strategies to facilitate student involvement at each cognitive level: knowledge, comprehension, application, analysis, synthesis, and evaluation. The strategies selected by the teacher create the opportunity for students to develop thinking skills at each cognitive level.

1   2   3   4   5   6   7   8   9

4.8   *Teachers implement strategies to facilitate student activities for each learning style.* Four major learning styles are reported continually in educational research: concrete-sequential thinking (hands on and step by step), abstract-random thinking (auditory and nonsequential), abstract-sequential thinking (written and step by step), and con-crete-random thinking (hands on and nonsequential). Each student-learning expectation is taught in multiple ways to enable students to learn through these different learning styles. The learning environment is designed with differ-ent learning stations allowing alternative learning-style instruction for students.

1   2   3   4   5   6   7   8   9

4.9   *Teachers pace the sequence and determine the scope and depth of the lesson to enhance student learning.* The order and depth given to instruction are critical to the student's ability to learn. Each student has his or her own time schedule for learning. Sequence and depth of instructional materials are designed to cover the student expectations. Different student abilities and capacities are met through the appropriate planning and implementing of sequenc-ing and pacing instruction. Also, the depth to which each student studies the learning expectations is determined by his or her ability and capacity. The teachers address all of these factors in the planning of instructional lessons.

1   2   3   4   5   6   7   8   9

4.10   *Teachers provide guided practice to determine student learning or need for reteaching.* After the teacher com-pletes instruction on new material, time is given for students to practice what they have learned. This prac-tice time is guided by the teacher to determine whether or not the student meets or possibly exceeds academic expectations or needs additional instruction to encour-age learning. Based on the teacher's findings, different learning-style materials and pacing may be implemented to enhance student learning. Assessing the student's knowledge through guided practice is critical for decid-ing the next move to benefit growth.

1   2   3   4   5   6   7   8   9

5.0   Assessment System

5.1   *Professional staff understand assessment is the evaluation of the instruction system.* The staff understand that
assessment is critical to the continual improvement of
instruction, which in turn improves student-learning opportunities. The assessment system gathers and analyzes
data and recommends strategies to improve instruction.

1   2   3   4   5   6   7   8   9

5.2   *Professional staff use various strategies to assess student learning.* Student learning is assessed through
various strategies. Some of the strategies teachers use to
assess student performance are paper-and-pencil tests,
oral reports, written reports, individual projects, team
projects, community work, and other contract agreements. The student portfolio includes multiple assessment data to give a diverse perspective of the student's
ability and capacity.

1   2   3   4   5   6   7   8   9

5.3   *Professional staff gather data on instructional strategies.*
Staff cooperate to gather and analyze data on instructional
strategies. Analyzing instructional-strategy data leads to
investigating the relationship between instructional strategies and student learning. Studying this relationship may
lead to revising instruction to improve student learning
and performance.

1   2   3   4   5   6   7   8   9

5.4   *Professional staff gather data on student curricular performance.* Student academic performance data are gathered and analyzed to assess the results of the instructional
program. This data analysis allows the faculty to judge
whether or not the instructional system is improving and
meeting academic expectations. This assessment is criti-

cal to the continual improvement of the entire academic program and is the lifeblood of the schooling process.

| 1 | 2 | 3 | 4 | 5 | 6 | 7 | 8 | 9 |

5.5   *Professional staff analyze academic data using statistical-analysis concepts.* Student-performance data are analyzed using statistical concepts. This analysis enables the staff to understand the system of instruction with respect to common causes of variation and special causes of variation. Common variation always exists within the system because it is built into the system itself. When only common causes of variation exist in the system, past system performance can predict future behavior. Special variation is not part of the normal process and causes the process to be unpredictable. When special variation exists, it is excessive and can be assigned to a specific cause. Statistical analysis of data allows the staff to understand these types of variations in order to predict and improve instructional strategies and student performance.

| 1 | 2 | 3 | 4 | 5 | 6 | 7 | 8 | 9 |

5.6   *Professional staff share academic analysis and findings with all faculty.* After data are gathered and analyzed, the staff share their findings with the entire staff to enable additional discussion and improvement of instruction. Everyone on the faculty is working on the instructional system to improve it. Unless everyone has knowledge of the data analysis and findings, it is not possible to be part of the improvement process.

| 1 | 2 | 3 | 4 | 5 | 6 | 7 | 8 | 9 |

5.7   *Professional staff use academic findings to improve instructional strategies.* If the findings from the data analysis suggest better instructional strategies with respect to specific student academic expectations, the faculty implement these changes. However, if the findings from the data analysis determine that certain instructional practices are not productive, they need to be discontinued. In either case, the aim is to continually improve the instructional system through data-based analysis.

1   2   3   4   5   6   7   8   9

5.8   *Professional staff share academic findings with their community partners.* The staff continually provide school community members with updates on academic progress with respect to changes in the instructional strategies and student-performance results.

1   2   3   4   5   6   7   8   9

5.9   *Professional staff involve community partners in the school-improvement process.* The staff not only share the academic data, analysis, and findings with community members, they also invite community partners to discuss future school academic priorities and concerns. This relationship with the community partners is continual and supports a learning community spirit. Without community support for the academic-improvement process and involvement in the school academic-improvement planning process, neither of these efforts can be successful or effective.

1   2   3   4   5   6   7   8   9

5.10   *Professional staff use recommendations to revise the school-improvement plan.* Based on the recommendations from the school-improvement process, priorities are identified and included in the future school-improvement plan. Priorities are stated in terms of staff-development strategies that help staff improve student learning and performance with respect to these priorities.

1   2   3   4   5   6   7   8   9

Decision-Making Process

CONTINUAL-IMPROVEMENT INTERVENTION PROCESS FOR COMMUNITY INVOLVEMENT AND PROFESSIONAL STAFF TO IMPROVE THE ACADEMIC SYSTEMS: DECISION MAKING– PROCESS CAUSES AND SOLUTIONS

The planning teams—whether at the community-involvement level or the professional-staff level—all use the same process and are an essential element in the continual-improvement philosophy. These teams are the backbone of the improvement process. At the community level, this team assists in identifying future school-improvement priorities. At the professional-staff level, these teams gather data and suggest new and better instructional strategies to continually improve the academic systems. It is important that these planning teams be organized with people who are invested in the areas being investigated. Also, adequate time needs to be given to the teams to understand the issues and concerns with respect to the improvement implementation. Administrative support is essential for these teams to achieve their goals.

The school continual-improvement process is based on the foundation of agreed-upon academic priorities. The key elements of this system are the parents, community leaders, teachers, administrators, and students themselves. Each year the school community needs to identify its priorities for the next academic year. The priority-identification system includes a number of process steps that enable each person to participate and be of value.

Representative samples of each of the population groups are invited to a series of meetings to identify school-improvement priorities, as are all the faculty and administrative staff of the building. Groups of five to seven members are selected who represent a mixture of the community groups. The groups follow a process that enables them to list and identify school-improvement priorities with little or no conflict. The groups are led through this process by a facilitator, and all groups proceed through the *decision making–process system* delineated below.

Decision Making–Process System

Issues-Identification and Root-Causes Analysis

1.0   Groups are selected (five to seven in a group) as stated above.

2.0   Groups brainstorm priority issues for improvement by writing each idea on a 5" × 8" index card using large felt pens, one idea per card (*no talking allowed*). The reason no talking is allowed is that each person must be allowed to think of ideas without being influenced by another person's comments during this step in the process.

3.0   After each and all members of the group have finished writing issues on cards, one member places his or her cards on the floor following the procedures listed below:

   3.1   Place a card down on the floor. Place the next card under it if it is related to the above card.

   3.2   If the idea on the next card is not related to the card previously put on the floor, start a new column.

   3.3   Proceed under this criterion until the person places all his or her cards on the floor.

   3.4   The next person in the group follows the same criterion and proceeds until all group members have their cards down on the floor in columns.

   3.5   *No talking allowed during this entire process.* Again, each person must be allowed to think without being influenced by another person during this step in the process.

4.0   Each of the above columns is analyzed as to its cause-and-effect relationship within the items contained in the column.

5.0   The column cards are numbered from 1, 2, 3 . . .

6.0   The group answers one question starting with the #1 card. Does the issue on the #1 card "cause" the issue on the #2 card? If the answer is yes, draw an arrow from 1 to 2. If the answer is no, do not draw an arrow and ask the same question of the #1 card with respect to the #3 card. Continue this process until #1 is analyzed with respect to all the cards on the table. After #1 is finished, do the same process with the #2 card with respect to all the other cards. Continue this process with all the issue cards on the table.

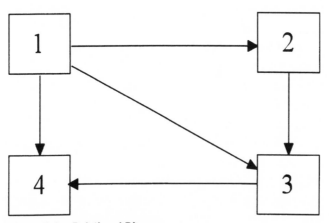

Figure B.1.   Relational Diagram

7.0   Determine which card has the most arrows coming from it and which card has the most arrows coming to it. The card(s) with the most arrows coming from it is (are) the root cause(s) of the issues on the table. The card(s) with the most arrows coming to it is (are) the result(s) of many of the other issues on the table. The issue identified as the *root cause* of most of the others is the one the staff need to identify in each issues column.

8.0   All of the *root causes* from the issues columns are now placed in a circle, as was done in the earlier process, and are analyzed as to the *super root causes* of the issues identified.

9.0   When the *super root causes* are identified, move to the next step:

Improvement Strategies–Planning Process to Determine Solutions

10.0 Groups brainstorm improvement strategies with respect to the super root causes identified through the root-cause process by writing each idea on a 5" × 8" index card using large felt pens, one idea per card (*no talking allowed*).

11.0 After all members of the group have finished writing ideas on cards, one member places his or her cards on the floor using the following procedures:

    11.1 Place a card down on the floor. Place the next card under it if it is related to the above card.

    11.2 If the idea on the next card is not related to the card previously put on the floor, start a new column. Proceed under this criterion until the person places all his or her cards on the floor.

    11.3 The next person in the group follows the same criterion and proceeds until all group members have their cards down on the floor in columns.

    11.4 *No talking is allowed during this entire process* (for the same reason as stated before).

12.0 After everyone has placed cards on the floor, anyone can now move any card to any place in any column where it is felt to be more related. Everyone is allowed to discuss the card moves and debate any move. This process is time consuming and should not be rushed. It is the key time for everyone to explain ideas and hear different points of view. The facilitator moves the discussion along but does not cut people off or force a decision. Respect for each person's view is critical, and *discussion is critical*! The facilitator reminds the group to remove any duplicate cards and to clarify any card that is not clear to the entire group.

13.0 After all the cards have been moved and the group is satisfied with the location of the cards, the group creates a title card for each column. Mark the title card, and number code the cards in each column so they are identified. Title cards are numbered 1.0, 2.0, and 3.0 . . . Cards under 1.0 are numbered 1.1, 1.2, and 1.3 . . . Cards under 2.0 are numbered 2.1, 2.2, 2.3 . . . and so on for all the cards. (*A cause-and-effect diagram can display this.*)

14.0   The next step is to determine which items are the most critical to the group at this time from all the causes generated. This is done through a multivoting process. The facilitator explains the criterion used for the voting process: If the item is *critical to be addressed now*, vote five fingers, if it is "important to be addressed now," vote 3 fingers. If it is *important but not critical at this time*, vote one finger. The facilitator reads each card and asks for the vote. All members of the group vote at the same time, and there is no talking during the voting process. The facilitator records the vote on each individual card. The facilitator reads the card, calls for the vote, and records the vote count on the card. This process is done on all the cards on the table but not on the title cards.

15.0   The top-voted cards are identified. The group might notice a natural break in the votes between the top level and the next level and select the top-level items.

16.0   These items are set in a column for the group to see and are labeled A, B, C, D, E, F, and so on. Then individuals in the group are asked to rank the items in order of importance to be addressed with the highest number given to the one *most critical* and the lowest number given to the *least critical* of the items in the column at this time.

17.0   The facilitator totals the *rank votes* and displays them on the board or overhead for all to see. Once the rank-vote totals are complete, ranking the items is next. The rank of the items is written next to the total vote column, and everyone can see the rank. If any items tie for a rank position, revote the item by the 5-3-1 method only to determine rank position and not to change its previously recorded total vote.

18.0   After the rank is recorded, the group determines whether or not the group has control over the items listed and ranked. The control analysis is done by asking the group whether or not it feels it has control over improving this item. The vote is done by the thumbs-up/thumbs-down method. If an individual feels the group has control over improving this item, vote thumbs up; if not, vote thumbs down. The facilitator records the control vote in the next column in the following manner: *yes* vote (5) / *no* vote (2) if seven people are in the group. After the control vote is recorded, the group may decide to discuss the control-vote interpretation and may vote again after some group clarification on the issue.

19.0   The rule that determines the group's priority to be addressed is *highest rank and highest control*. The items with the highest rank and highest control are the items the group feels are the best ones they can do something about at the present time. This is where the group feels the best chance of success is at this time.

20.0   The same *decision-making process* can now be used to create ideas and strategies for the school-improvement implementation plan on the items to be improved. The team that is assigned to a particular item can use this process to help itself address the improvement-planning process and design the plan and implementation steps.

21.0   Select a planning team to plan the implementation of the determined solution. This planning team uses the *plan-do-study-act cycle* to move forward on the solution implementation.

Decision Making–Process Outline and Flowcharts and Plan-Do-Study-Act Cycle Outline and Flowchart

Identifying Causes Preventing Process Aim

1.0   Draw flowchart of present process if it exists.

2.0   Brainstorm causes preventing the aim written on 5" × 8" cards (*no talking*).

3.0   Cluster, clarify, and remove duplicate causes with open discussion and debate.

4.0   Create header card for each column of causes.

5.0   Create cause-and-effect diagram (fishbone).

6.0   Analyze each column for root causes using arrow method.

7.0   Select *super* root causes from root causes.

8.0   Analyze control of causes selected (*no talking*, thumbs up/thumbs down). After vote, discuss, and revote control if necessary.

9.0   Select causes to be addressed based on highest root cause, highest rank, and highest control. Causes not controlled are assigned to other agendas.

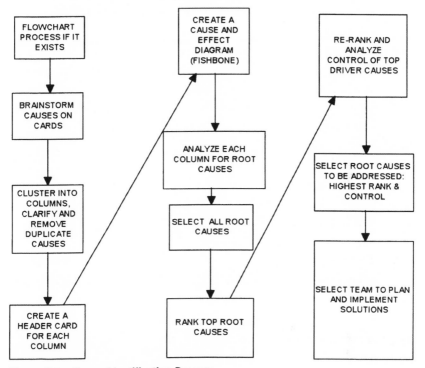

Figure B.2.   *Cause-Identification Process*

Solution Planning and Implementing

10.0   Brainstorm solutions.

11.0   Cluster, clarify, and remove duplicate solutions.

12.0   Create header card for each column of solutions.

13.0   Create solution and result diagram (fishbone).

14.0   Vote (5-3-1) each solution, not including title card.

15.0   Select top cluster of solutions based on vote.

16.0   Rank solutions selected.

17.0   Analyze control of solutions selected.

18.0   Solutions controlled are analyzed for driving solution.

19.0   Solutions not controlled are assigned to other agendas.

20.0   Select driving solution to be addressed and solved.

21.0   Select team to plan and implement solution.

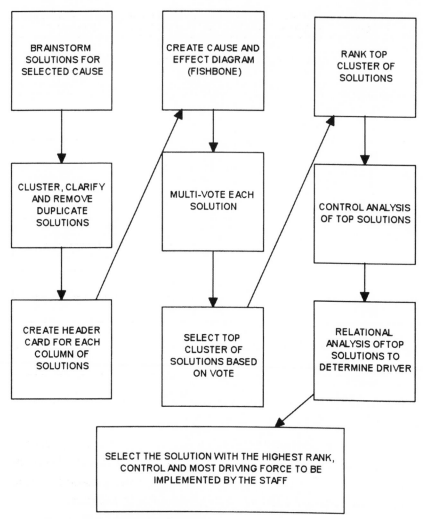

Figure B.3.   Solution-Planning Process

TOP SELECTED ITEMS	RANK SCORES				RANK TOTALS	RANK #	CONTROL #YES/#NO	TASK SELECTION PRIORITY
ITEM	1	2	3	4	R T	#	YES/NO	HIGHEST RANK AND CONTROL
A								
B								
C								
D								
E								
F								
G								
H								
I								
J								
(...)								

Figure B.4. Ranking Process and Control Analysis

In the following *plan-do-study-act cycle*, the faculty use the *decision making–process system* described in appendix B to identify improvement priorities. The planning team implements the plan-do-study-act cycle by addressing the following steps and items in each step:

Plan the intervention to be implemented, and select the people to implement the intervention.

   1. Who is doing the implementation?
   2. Where is the implementation expanded?
   3. How is the implementation designed?
   4. What are the expected criteria?
   5. How are the criteria assessed?
   6. How are new data collected?
   7. How are new data to be analyzed?

8. When are new data shared?
9. With whom are data shared?
10. What are the recommendations?

Do the implementation of the intervention.

1. The instructional methods are implemented.
2. Research group is identified.
3. Control group is identified.
4. Time limits are established.
5. Criteria are established.
6. Data-collection methods are identified.
7. Data-collection times are determined.

Study the assessment data from the intervention.

1. Data are analyzed.
2. Findings are determined.
3. Conclusions are stated.
4. Recommendations are suggested.
5. Impact of recommendations is analyzed.
6. Integration of recommendations is considered.
7. Final recommendations are agreed upon.

Act on the final improvement recommendations.

1. Plan staff development on the intervention.
2. Support staff with mentoring and modeling.
3. Expand the intervention implementation.
4. Plan assessment of the implementation.
5. Assess the implementation.
6. Continually assess and improve the implementation.

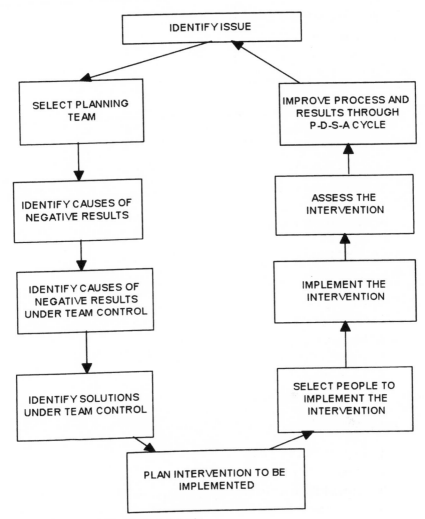

Figure B.5.   Plan-Do-Study-Act Cycle

References

INTRODUCTION

Sekulich, K. 2000. *The relationship between school improvement and student achievement*. PhD Diss, National Louis University.

CHAPTER 1

Deming, W. E. 1994. *The new economics for industry, government, education*. 2nd ed. Cambridge, MA: MIT Center for Advanced Engineering Study.

Bloom, B. 1956. *Taxonomy of educational objectives*. New York: David McKay.

Webster's new collegiate dictionary. 1980. Springfield, MA: G. & C. Merriam Co.

Tomal, D. 2010. *Action research for educators*. 2nd ed. Lanham, MD: Rowman & Littlefield Education.

http://www.kuwongbss.qld.edu.au/thinking/Bloom/blooms.htm

Creswell, J. 1998. *Quantitative inquiry and research design: Choosing among five traditions*. Thousand Oaks, CA: Sage.

Wheeler, D. 1992. *Understanding statistical process control*. 2nd. ed. Knoxville: SPC Press, Inc.

Warwick, R. 1995. *Beyond piecemeal improvements: How to transform your school using Deming's quality principles*. Bloomington, IN: National Educational Service.

SPC-IV. 2014. *Statistical process control, control chart data analysis*. Tucson, AZ: Quality America, Inc. Retrieved from www.qualityamerica.com/ SPC_Software.asp, July 15, 2014.

CHAPTER 2

Adams, C. Should all schools be virtual? *Scholastic*. October 6, 2013. http://www.scholastic.com/browse/article.jsp?id=3751959.

http://online.sfsu.edu/rpurser/revised/pages/problem.htm (accessed February 2, 2014).

http://en.wikipedia.org/wiki/Project-lead-the-Way (accessed February 11, 2014).

iNACOL. 2011. Online learning: Virtual schools accountability issues brief. Brief. Vienna, VA: iNACOL. Text available online at http://www.doe.virginia.gov/boe/meetings/2013/work_session/03_mar/work_session_brief_inacol.pdf.

Illinois State Board of Education. n.d. Performance Evaluation Reform Act (PERA) and Senate Bill 7. http://www.isbe.net/PERA/default.htm, January 2010.

Cuban, Larry, ed. 2013. Virtual schools in the U.S. 2013: Politics, performance, policy, and research evidence. Boulder: National Education Policy Center and the School of Education, University of Colorado, Boulder. http://nepc.colorado.edu/files/nepc-virtual-2013.pdf.

Horn, M. B. 2013. Digital learning and state legislatures. *EducationNext* (August 12), http://educationnext.org/digital-learning-and-state-legislatures/.

Headden, S. 2013. The promise of personalized learning. *EducationNext* 13 (4) (Fall), http://educationnext.org/the-promise-of-personalized-learning/.

iNACOL. 2006. Top ten myths about virtual schools. Brief. Vienna, VA: iNACOL. http://www.inacol.org/cms/wp-content/uploads/2013/04/TenMythsAboutVirtualSchools.pdf.

Warwick, R. 1995. *Beyond piecemeal improvements: How to transform your school using Deming's quality principles*. Bloomington, IN: National Educational Service.

Hattie, J. 2009. *Visible learning: A synthesis of over 800 meta-analyses relating to achievement*. London, New York: Routledge.

Warwick, R. 1995. *Beyond piecemeal improvements: How to transform your school using Deming's quality principles*. Bloomington, IN: National Educational Service.

Warwick, R. 2010. *School academic system improvement using data analysis*. Notebook used for teaching graduate classes. Lakemoor, IL.

CHAPTER 4

Warwick, R. 1995. *Beyond piecemeal improvements: How to transform your school using Deming's quality principles*. Bloomington, IN: National Educational Service.

Revised Bloom's Taxonomy, http://www.utar.edu.ny/file/Revised_Blooms/Info.pdf (accessed July 15, 2014).

Warwick, R. 2010. *School academic system improvement using data analysis*. Notebook used for teaching graduate classes. Lakemoor, IL.

bie.org (accessed 2014).

San Francisco State University. n.d. Problem-based learning. http://online.sfsu.edu/rpurser/revised/pages/problem.htm (accessed February 2, 2014).

David, Jane L. *What research says about project-based learning*, http://www.ascd.org/publications/educational_leadership/feb08/vol65/num05/Project-Based_Learning.aspx (accessed February 2, 2014).

CHAPTER 5

Joyce, B., and B. Showers. 1983. *Power in staff development through research on training*. Alexandria, VA: ASCD.

Gregoric, A. F. 1979. Learning/teaching styles: Potent forces behind them. *Educational Leadership* 36 (4): 234–36.

Marzano, J., D. J. Pickering, and J. E. Pollock. 2005. *Classroom instruction that works: Research based strategies for increasing student achievement*. Alexandria, VA: ASCD.

Warwick, R. 2010. *School academic system improvement using data analysis*. Notebook used for teaching graduate classes. Lakemoor, IL.

Study Guides and Strategies. 1996. Cooperative learning strategies: Problem-based learning. http://www.studygs.net/pbl.htm (accessed February 11, 2014).

CHAPTER 6

Wheeler, D. 1992. *Understanding statistical process control*. 2nd ed. Knoxville: SPC Press, Inc.

Wheeler, D. 1993. *Understanding variation: The key to managing chaos*. Knoxville: SPC Press, Inc.

Warwick, R. 1995. *Beyond piecemeal improvements: How to transform your school using Deming's quality principles*. Bloomington, IN: National Educational Service.

SPC-IV (2014). Statistical process control, control chart data analysis. Tucson, AZ: Quality America, Inc. Retrieved from: www.qualityamerica.com/SPC_Software.asp, July 2014.

Revised Bloom's Taxonomy, http://www.utar.edu.ny/file/Revised_Blooms/Info.pdf (accessed July 15, 2014).

CHAPTER 7

Warwick, R. 1995. *Beyond piecemeal improvements: How to transform your school using Deming's quality principles*. Bloomington, IN: National Educational Service.

About the Author

Ron Warwick is professor of Educational Leadership at Concordia University, Chicago, and has been involved in the educational profession for over fifty years. He has been a teacher, administrator, and consultant during this time. He taught high school mathematics in Chicago Public Schools and in the Indiana University Upward Bound Program. He was an assistant professor at Toledo University and was a professor as well as department chair at National Louis University and now holds a teaching position at Concordia University.

His administrative experience includes responsibilities as a middle-school principal, associate superintendent of curriculum and instruction, and chair of the Educational Leadership Department for over twenty years. In addition to his roles as teacher and administrator, he has consulted with school systems, state departments, and other educational organizations. Ron has published over twenty articles in educational journals, numerous booklets, and a book and has been involved in a number of research and grant projects. He has been invited to present his leadership ideas throughout the United States, Europe, and South Korea.

Warwick received a B.S. in mathematics and an M.Ed. in education from Loyola University, Chicago. In 1968 he received an Ed.D. in administration and curriculum from Indiana University, Bloomington. Postdoctoral studies include the individually guided education concept through the multiunit-school design supported by the Sloan Kettering Foundation through the work of Dr. John Goodlad in the late 1960s and 1970s. Additional studies include the situational-leadership theory in the 1980s with Dr. Ken Blanchard's leadership organization and the continual-improvement philosophy with Dr. W. Edwards Deming through his seminars in the early 1990s.